1·2·3 Skein Crochet

Edited by Judy Crow

HOUSE of
WHITE
BIRCHES

PUBLISHERS
SINCE 1947

1·2·3 Skein Crochet

Editor *Judy Crow*
Art Director *Brad Snow*
Publishing Services Manager *Brenda Gallmeyer*

Assistant Art Directo *Nick Pierce*
Copy Supervisor *Michelle Beck*
Copy Editors *Amanda Ladig, Susanna Tobias*
Technical Editor *Mary Ann Frits*
Technical Artist *Nicole Gage, Pam Gregory*

Graphic Arts Supervisor *Ronda Bechinski*
Book Design *Nick Pierce*
Graphic Artists *Vicki Staggs, Jessi Butler*
Production Assistants *Marj Morgan, Judy Neuenschwander*

Photography *Scott Campbell*
Photography Assistant *Martha Coquat*

First Printing: 2009, China
Library of Congress Number: 2008923305
Hardcover ISBN: 978-1-59217-254-2
Softcover ISBN: 978-1-59217-255-9

DRGbooks.com

1 2 3 4 5 6 7 8 9

Welcome

· ·

Does your yarn stash grow larger each year? If you are like me, you can't stand to throw away those two or three leftover partial skeins or those bits and pieces of yarn from your last project. So you just pack them away thinking, "Someday I'll do something with these".

Well, it's time to bring out those boxes and bags of leftover yarn. Each design in this collection is not only fun to stitch, but also requires only three skeins of yarn or less. Let's do some spring cleaning, and use up those remnants from previous projects.

These designs are also perfect for testing the more costly yarns. My trips to the yarn store often leave me drooling over the more expensive yarn; however, on my budget, it simply isn't feasible to purchase enough for a large project. A project requiring 3 or less skeins can be very affordable—it's a wonderful way to try the more luxurious yarns.

Whether you are using up the old or trying some new yarns, we've put together a great selection of designs just for family, just for home and just for fun.

Happy Stitching,

Judy Crow

Contents

Just for Men

Surprise the man in your life with a crocheted gift. These handmade hats, slippers, pillows and more will make him feel really special.

Man's Slippers

Design by *Jewdy Lambert*

Finished Sizes
One size fits most

Materials
• NaturallyCaron.com
Country medium
(worsted) weight yarn
(3 oz/185 yds/
85g per skein):
  2 skeins #0023
  chocolate truffle
• Medium (worsted)
weight yarn:
  3 yds variegated
• Size I/9/5.5mm crochet
hook or size needed to
obtain gauge
• Tapestry needle

Gauge
4 sts = 1 inch

Pattern Notes
Weave in ends as work progresses.

Join with slip stitch as indicated unless otherwise stated.

Chain-3 at beginning of row or round counts as first double crochet unless otherwise stated.

Slipper

Make 2.

Toe

Rnd 1 (RS): With chocolate truffle, ch 4, **join** (*see Pattern Notes*) in first ch to form a ring, **ch 3** (*see Pattern Notes*), 17 dc in ring, join in 3rd ch of beg ch-3, turn. (*18 dc*)

Rnd 2: Ch 3, dc in same ch as joining, 2 dc in each dc around, join in 3rd ch of beg ch-3, turn. (*36 dc*)

Rnd 3: Ch 3, **fpdc** (see Stitch Guide) around each of next 2 dc, ***bpdc** (see Stitch Guide) around each of next 3 dc, fpdc around each of next 3 dc, rep from * around to last 3 dc, bpdc around each of last 3 dc, join in 3rd ch of beg ch-3.

Rnd 4: Ch 3, fpdc around each of next 2 sts, *bpdc around each of next 3 sts, fpdc around each of next 3 sts, rep from * around to last 3 sts, bpdc around each of last 3 sts, join in 3rd ch of beg ch-3.

Rnd 5: Rep rnd 4.

Rnd 6: Ch 3, bpdc around each of next 2 dc, *fpdc around each of next 3 dc, bpdc around each of next 3 dc, rep from * around to last 3 sts, fpdc around each of last 3 sts, join in 3rd ch of beg ch-3.

Rnds 7 & 8: Rep rnd 6.

Rnds 9–11: Rep rnds 3–5.

Rnds 12–14: Rep rnds 6–8.

Rnds 15–21: Rep rnds 9–14. At end of last rnd, fasten off.

Cuff

Row 1 (RS): Hold piece with RS facing, join chocolate truffle in sp between 15th and 16th st of last rnd, ch 6, fasten off. Rejoin chocolate truffle in 19th st of same rnd, ch 9, dc in 4th ch from hook (beg 3 sk chs count as a dc), dc in each of next 4 chs, sk next ch, fpdc around same st as joining sl st made, fpdc around each of next 2 sts, *bpdc around each of next 3 sts, fpdc around each of next 3 sts, rep from * to last 6 chs, dc in each of last 6 chs (mark first dc made), turn. (45 sts)

Row 2: Ch 3, bpdc around each of next 2 dc, *fpdc around each of next 3 dc, bpdc around each of next 3 sts, rep from * 5 times, fpdc around each of next 3 sts, bpdc around each of next 2 sts, dc in 3rd ch of beg 3 sk chs, turn.

Row 3: Ch 3, fpdc around each of next 2 sts, *bpdc around each of next 3 sts, fpdc around each of next 3 sts, rep from * 5 times, bpdc around each of next 3 sts, fpdc around each of next 2 sts, dc in 3rd ch of beg ch-3, turn.

Row 4: Ch 3, bpdc around each of next 2 sts, *fpdc around each of next 3 dc, bpdc around each of next 3 sts, rep from * 5 times, fpdc around each of next 3 sts, bpdc around each of next 2 sts, dc in 3rd ch of beg ch-3, turn.

Rows 5–12: [Rep rows 3 and 4 alternately] 4 times. At end of last row, fasten off.

Edging

Hold Cuff with WS facing, join variegated in ch at base of marked dc on row 1 of Cuff, sc in each ch to last ch, 2 sc in last ch, sc evenly sp across edge of Cuff to next corner, 2 sc in corner, working across next side, sc in each ch across. Fasten off. •

Pop Top Mittens

Design by *Donna Childs*

Skill Level

EASY

Size
One size fits most

Materials
• Brown Sheep Company Lamb's Pride Superwash medium (worsted) weight yarn (4 oz/200 yds/113g per skein):
   2 skeins #SW01 red wing
• Size G/6/4mm crochet hook or size needed to obtain gauge
• Tapestry needle

Gauge
19 sc = 4 inches; 20 rnds = 4 inches

Pattern Notes
Weave in ends as work progresses.

Join with slip stitch as indicated unless otherwise stated.

Chain-3 at beginning of row or round counts as first double crochet unless otherwise stated.

Mitten
Make 2.

Cuff

Rnd 1 (RS): Ch 36, **join** (*see Pattern Notes*) in first ch, taking care not to twist ch, **ch 3** (*see Pattern Notes*), dc in each rem ch around, join in 3rd ch of beg ch-3. (*36 dc*)

Rnd 2: Ch 3, **fpdc** (*see Stitch Guide*) around next dc, ***bpdc** (*see Stitch Guide*) around next dc, fpdc around next dc, rep from * around, join in 3rd ch of beg ch-3.

Rep rnd 2 until piece measures 2½ inches.

Last rnd: Ch 1, 2 sc in same ch as joining, sc in each dc around, join in beg sc. (*37 sc*)

Hand

Rnd 1: Ch 1, sc in each of first 17 sc, 2 sc in next sc, sc in next sc, 2 sc in next sc, sc in each of next 17 sc, join in beg sc. (*39 sc*)

Rnd 2: Ch 1, sc in each sc around, join in beg sc.

Rnd 3: Ch 1, sc in each of first 17 sc, 2 sc in next sc, sc in each of next 3 sc, 2 sc in next sc, sc in each of next 17 sc, join in beg sc. *(41 sc)*

Rnd 4: Rep rnd 2.

Rnd 5: Ch 1, sc in each of first 17 sc, 2 sc in next sc, sc in each of next 5 sc, 2 sc in next sc, sc in each of next 17 sc, join in beg sc. *(43 sc)*

Rnd 6: Rep rnd 2.

Rnd 7: Ch 1, sc in each of first 17 sc, 2 sc in next sc, sc in each of next 7 sc, 2 sc in next sc, sc in each of next 17 sc, join in beg sc. *(45 sc)*

Rnd 8: Rep rnd 2.

Rnd 9: Ch 1, sc in each of first 17 sc, 2 sc in next sc, sc in each of next 9 sc, 2 sc in next sc, sc in each of next 17 sc, join in beg sc. *(47 sc)*

Rnd 10: Rep rnd 2.

Rnd 11: Ch 1, sc in each of first 17 sc, 2 sc in next sc, sc in each of next 11 sc, 2 sc in next sc, sc in each of next 17 sc, join in beg sc. *(49 sc)*

Rnd 12: Rep rnd 2.

Rnd 13: Ch 1, sc in each of first 17 sc, 2 sc in next sc, sc in each of next 13 sc, 2 sc in next sc, sc in each of next 17 sc, join in beg sc. *(51 sc)*

Rnd 14: Rep rnd 2.

Rnd 15: Ch 1, sc in each of first 18 sc, ch 1, sk next 15 sc *(gusset)*, sc in each of next 18 sc, join in beg sc. *(37 sts)*

Rnd 16: Ch 1, sc in each st around, join in beg sc.

Rnds 17–25: Rep rnd 2. At end of last rnd, fasten off.

Continued on page 29

Man's Hat & Scarf

Designs by *Lisa Gentry*

. . . .

Finished Size
Hat: 8 inches long x 22 inches in circumference
Scarf: Approximately 5¾ x 66 inches

Materials
Hat
• Red Heart Soft Yarn medium (worsted) weight yarn (5 oz/256 yds/140g per skein):
  2 skeins #4614 black
  1 skein #1882 toast
• Size I/9/5.5mm crochet hook or size needed to obtain gauge
• Tapestry needle
Scarf
• Red Heart Soft Yarn medium (worsted) weight yarn (5 oz/256 yds/140g per skein):
  2 skeins #4614 black
  1 skein #1882 toast
• Size I/9/5.5mm crochet hook or size needed to obtain gauge
• Tapestry needle

Man's Hat
Gauge
In pattern: 15 sts = 4 inches; 11 rnds = 4 inches

Pattern Notes
Weave in ends as work progresses.

Join with slip stitch as indicated unless otherwise stated.

Chain-3 at beginning of row or round counts as first double crochet unless otherwise stated.

Hat
Rnd 1 (RS): Beg at top and with black, ch 4, **join** *(see Pattern Notes)* in first ch to form a ring, **ch 3** *(see Pattern Notes)*, 11 dc in ring, join in 3rd ch of beg ch-3. *(12 dc)*

Rnd 2: Ch 1, 2 sc in same ch as joining, 2 sc in each rem dc around, join in beg sc. *(24 sc)*

Rnd 3: Ch 3, 2 dc in next sc, *dc in next sc, 2 dc in next sc, rep from * around, join in 3rd ch of beg ch-3. *(36 dc)*

Rnd 4: Ch 1, sc in same ch as joining, sc in next dc, 2 sc in next dc, *sc in each of next 2 dc, 2 sc in next dc, rep from * around, join in beg sc. *(48 sc)*

Rnd 5: Ch 3, dc in each of next 2 sc, 2 dc in next sc, *dc in each of next 3 sc, 2 dc in next sc, rep from * around, join in 3rd ch of beg ch-3. *(60 dc)*

Rnd 6: Ch 1, sc in each of first 4 dc, 2 sc in next dc, *sc in each of next 4 sc, 2 sc in next sc, rep from * around, join in beg sc. (72 sc)

Rnd 7: Ch 3, dc in each sc around, join in 3rd ch of beg ch-3.

Rnd 8: Ch 1, sc in each dc around, join in beg sc.

Rows 9–18: [Rep rows 7 and 8 alternately] 5 times, **changing color** (*see Stitch Guide*) to toast in last sc of last rnd.

Row 19: Ch 1, sc in each of first 2 sc, ***fpdc** (*see Stitch Guide*) loosely around next sc on 2nd row below, sc in each of next 5 sc, rep from * 10 times, fpdc around next sc on 2nd row below, sc in each of next 3 sc, join in beg sc.

Rnd 20: Rep rnd 7, changing to black in last dc.

Rnd 21: Ch 1, sc in each of first 2 sc, *work 1 fpdc around fpdc two rows down, sc in each of next 5 sc, rep from * 10 more times, work 1 fpdc around fpdc two rows down, sc in each of last 3 sc, join in beg ch-1.

Rnd 22: Rep rnd 7, changing to toast in last dc.

Rnd 23: Rep rnd 21.

Continued on page 30

Manly Afghan

Design by *Cynthia Adams*

Skill Level

EASY

Finished Size
40 inches x 38 inches

Materials
• Caron One Pound Jumbo Prints medium (worsted) weight yarn (10 oz/ 507 yds/284g per skein):
   3 skeins #563 mixed greens ombre
• Size I/9/5.5mm crochet hook or size needed to obtain gauge
• Tapestry needle

Gauge
8 dc = 3 inches

Pattern Notes
Weave in ends as work progresses.

Chain-2 at beginning of row or round counts as first double crochet unless otherwise stated.

Afghan
Row 1: Ch 116, dc in 3rd ch from hook (*beg 2 sk chs count as first dc*), dc in each rem ch across, turn.

Row 2: Ch 2 (*see Pattern Notes*), **fpdc** (*see Stitch Guide*) around each of next 2 dc, **bpdc** (*see Stitch Guide*) around next dc, *fpdc around each of next 3 dc, bpdc around next dc, rep from * across to last 3 sts, fpdc around each of next 2 dc, dc in 2nd ch of beg 2 sk chs, turn.

Row 3: Ch 2, dc in each of next 2 sts, *fpdc around next st, dc in each of next 3 sts, rep from * across to last 4 sts, fpdc around next st, dc in each of next 2 sts, dc in 2nd ch of beg ch-2, turn.

Row 4: Ch 2, fpdc around each of next 2 sts, bpdc around next st, *fpdc around each of next 3 sts, bpdc around next st, rep from * across to last 3 sts, fpdc around each of next 2 sts, dc in 2nd ch of beg ch-2, turn.

Rep rows 3 and 4 alternately until piece measures 38 inches from beg, ending with row 3. At end of last row, **do not turn**.

Edging

Ch 1, working left to right across last row, work **reverse sc** (*see Fig. 1*) in each st across, working across next side in ends of rows, work 3 reverse sc in each row across, working across next side in unused lps of starting ch, reverse sc in each lp across, working across next side in ends of rows, work 3 reverse sc in each row across to beg reverse sc, join with sl st in beg reverse sc. Fasten off. ●

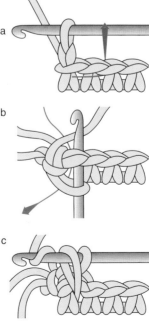

Fig 1.
Reverse Single Crochet

Man's Camo Hat & Scarf

Designs by *Glenda Winkleman*

Size

Hat: One size fits most
Scarf: 5¼ inches x 66 inches

Materials

Hat
• Red Heart Classic medium (worsted) weight yarn (3 oz/146 yds/85g per skein):
  2 skeins #971 camouflage
• Size I/9/5.5mm crochet hook or size needed to obtain gauge
• Tapestry needle

Scarf
• Red Heart Classic medium (worsted) weight yarn (3 oz/146 yds/85g per skein):
  3 skeins #971 camouflage
• Size I/9/5.5mm crochet hook or size needed to obtain gauge
• Tapestry needle

Man's Camo Hat

Gauge

Rnds 1 & 2 = 1½ inches

Pattern Note

Weave in ends as work progresses.

Hat

Note: Hat is worked in continuous rounds. Do not join unless specified; mark beginning of rounds.

Rnd 1 (RS): Beg at top, ch 2, 6 sc in 2nd ch from hook. *(6 dc)*

Rnd 2: (Sc, dc) in each sc around. *(12 sts)*

Rnd 3: *(Sc, dc) in next sc, sc in next dc, rep from * around. *(18 sts)*

Rnd 4: (Sc, dc) in next sc, sc in next dc, *dc in next sc, (sc, dc) in next sc, sc in next dc, rep from * around to last sc, dc in last sc. *(24 sts)*

Rnd 5: Rep rnd 3. *(36 sts at end of rnd)*

Rnd 6: Rep rnd 4. *(48 sts at end of rnd)*

Rnd 7: *(Sc, dc) in next sc, sc in next dc, dc in next sc, sc in next dc, rep from * around *(60 sts)*

Rnd 8: *Dc in next st, sc in next st, rep from * around.

Continued on page 31

Travel Pillows

Design by Elaine Bartlett

Finished Size
Neck Pillow: 12 inches x 14 inches

Square Pillow: 9 inches x 12 inches

Materials
Neck Pillow
• Red Heart Super Saver medium (worsted) weight yarn (solids: 7 oz/364 yds/198g per skein; multis: 5 oz/244 yds/141g per skein):
   1 skein each
   #380 Windsor blue
   and #794 bay print
• Size H/8/5mm crochet hook or size needed to obtain gauge
• Tapestry needle
• Polyester fiberfill
• Stitch marker

Square Pillow
• Red Heart Super Saver medium (worsted) weight yarn (solids: 7 oz/364 yds/198g per skein; multis: 5 oz/244 yds/141g per skein):
   1 skein each
   #380 Windsor blue
   and #794 bay print
• Size H/8/5mm crochet hook or size needed to obtain gauge
• Tapestry needle
• Polyester fiberfill
• Stitch marker

Neck Travel Pillow
Gauge
12 sc = 4 inches; 16 sc rows = 4 inches

Pattern Note
Weave in ends as work progresses.

Pillow
Front/Back

Make 1 of each color.

Row 1 (RS): Beg at back edge, ch 21, sc in 2nd ch from hook, sc in each rem ch across, turn. *(20 sc)*

Row 2: Ch 1, 2 sc in first sc, sc in each sc across to last sc, 2 sc in last sc, turn. *(22 sc)*

Row 3: Ch 1, 2 sc in first sc, sc in each sc across to last sc, 2 sc in last sc, turn. *(24 sc)*

Row 4: Ch 1, sc in each sc across, turn.

Rows 5–16: [Rep rows 2–4 consecutively] 4 times. *(40 sc at end of last row)*

Rows 17–28: Rep row 4.

Row 29: Ch 1, sc in each of first 15 sc, leaving rem sc unworked, turn. *(15 sc)*

Rows 30–46: Rep row 4.

First Section

Row 47: Ch 1, **sc dec** (*see Stitch Guide*) in first 2 sc, sc in each sc across to last sc, 2 sc in last sc, turn. (*15 sc*)

Row 48: Ch 1, 2 sc in first sc, sc in each sc across to last 2 sc, sc dec in last 2 sc, turn. (*15 sc*)

Row 49: Rep row 4.

Row 50: Rep row 48.

Row 51: Rep row 47.

Row 52: Rep row 4.

Row 53: Ch 1, sc dec in first 2 sc, sc in each sc across to last 2 sc, sc dec in last 2 sc, turn. (*13 sc*)

Rows 54–58: Rep row 53. At end of last row, fasten off. (*3 sc at end of last row*)

2nd Section

Row 1: Hold piece with RS facing and row 46 at top, sk next 10 sc from First Section, join with sc in next sc, sc in each rem sc, turn. (*15 sc*)

Row 2: Ch 1, sc in each sc across, turn.

Rows 3–18: Rep row 2.

Row 19: Ch 1, 2 sc in first sc, sc in each sc across to last 2 sc, sc dec in last 2 sc, turn. (*15 sc*)

Row 20: Ch 1, sc dec in first 2 sc, sc in each sc across to last sc, 2 sc in last sc. (*15 sc*)

Row 21: Rep row 2.

Row 22: Rep row 20.

Row 23: Rep row 19.

Row 24: Rep row 2.

Row 25: Ch 1, sc dec in first 2 sc, sc in each sc across to last 2 sc, sc dec in last 2 sc, turn. (*13 sc*)

Rows 26–30: Rep row 25. At end of last row, fasten off. (*3 sc at end of last row*)

Strap

Row 1 (RS): With Windsor blue, ch 21, working in back bar of chs, sc in 2nd ch from hook, sc in each rem ch across, turn. (*20 sc*)

Continued on page 32

Camo Socks

Design by Jewdy Lambert

Sizes

Instructions given fit men's small (men's shoe sizes 6–7; changes for medium (men's shoe sizes (8–9) and large (men's shoe sizes 10–12) are in [ ].

Materials

• Red Heart Classic medium (worsted) weight yarn (3 oz/148 yds/ 85g per skein):
  2 skeins #971 camouflage
• Brown Sheep Company Lamb's Pride medium (worsted) weight yarn (4 oz/190 yds/ 113g per skein):
  1 oz/50 yds/28g M69 old sage
• Size I/9/5.5mm crochet hook or size needed to obtain gauge
• Tapestry needle

Gauge

4 sc = 1 inch; 3 dc = inch

Pattern Notes

Weave in ends as work progresses.

Join with slip stitch as indicated unless otherwise stated.

Chain-2 at beginning of row or round counts as first single crochet unless otherwise stated.

Chain-3 at beginning of row or round counts as first double crochet unless otherwise stated.

Sock

Make 2.

Cuff

Row 1 (RS): Ch 30, dc in 4th ch from hook, dc in each rem ch across, turn. *(23 dc)*

Row 2: Ch 3 *(see Pattern Notes)*, working in **back lps** *(see Stitch Guide)*, dc in each dc across, turn.

Rows 3–25: Rep row 2.

Row 26: Fold piece so starting ch is behind row 25, ch 1, working through dc on row 25 and corresponding unused lps of starting ch at same time, sc in each dc across. Fasten off.

Turn seam to WS.

Ankle

Note: *Joining forms center back seam.*

Rnd 1 (RS): Hold piece with RS facing and 1 long edge at top, **join** *(see Pattern Notes)* yarn in first sc to right of seam, ch 1, 2 sc in same sc, 2 sc in each rem sc around, join in beg sc. *(46 sc)*

Rnd 2: Ch 2 *(see Pattern Notes)*, sc in each sc across, turn.

Rnds 3–9: Rep rnd 2. At end of last rnd, fasten off.

Heel Flap

Row 1 (RS): Fold piece in half with Ankle joinings centered on top, join green in 8th sc to right of joining, ch 2, sc in each of next 15 sc, leaving rem sc unworked, turn. *(16 sc)*

Row 2: Ch 2, sc in each sc across, turn.

Rows 3–9: Rep row 2.

Row 10: Sk first sc, sl st in next sc, ch 2, sc in each of next 13 sc, leaving rem sc unworked, turn. *(14 sc)*

Row 11: Sk first sc, sl st in next sc, ch 2, sc in each of next 11 sc, leaving rem sc unworked, turn. *(12 sc)*

Row 12: Sk first sc, sl st in next sc, ch 2, sc in each of next 9 sc, leaving rem sc unworked, turn. *(10 sc)*

Row 13: Sk first sc, sl st in next sc, ch 2, sc in each of next 7 sc, leaving rem sc unworked, turn. *(8 sc)*

Row 14: Sk first sc, sl st in next sc, ch 2, sc in each of next 5 sc, leaving rem sc unworked. Fasten off. *(6 sc)*

Heel Turning

Rnd 1 (RS): Hold piece with RS facing, join camouflage in edge of row 1 of Heel Flap, ch 2, work 9 sc evenly sp across side of Heel Flap, working across row 14, sc in each sc across, work 10 sc evenly spaced across next side of Heel Flap, sc in each of next 16 unworked sc on rnd 6 of Ankle, join in 2nd ch of beg ch-2, turn. *(42 sc)*

Rnd 2: Ch 2, **sc dec** *(see Stitch Guide)* in next 2 sc, sc in each of next 21 sc, sc dec in next 2 sc, sc in each of next 16 sc, join in 2nd ch of beg ch-2, turn. *(40 sc)*

Continued on page 33

Blue/White Hat & Scarf

Designs by *Sheila Leslie*

. . . .

Skill Level
◼◼◻◻
EASY

Size
Hat: Fits adult man
Scarf: 7 inches x
49 inches

Finished Size
20 inches in
circumference

Materials
Hat
• Red Heart Super Saver
medium (worsted) weight
yarn (7 oz/364 yds/198g
per skein):
  1 skein #382
  country blue
  14 yds each #311 white
  and #387 soft navy
• Size H/8/5mm crochet
hook or size needed to
obtain gauge
• Tapestry needle
Scarf
• Red Heart Super Saver
medium (worsted) weight
yarn (7 oz/364 yds/198g
per skein):
  1 skein #382
  country blue
  9 yds each #311 white
  and #387 soft navy
• Size I/9/5.5mm crochet
hook or size needed to
obtain gauge
• Tapestry needle

Blue/White Hat
Gauge
4 sc = 1 inch

Pattern Note
Weave in ends as work progresses.

Join with slip stitch as indicated unless otherwise stated.

Hat
Cuff

Row 1 (RS): With country blue, ch 25, sc in 2nd ch from hook, sc in each rem ch across, turn. *(24 sc)*

Row 2: Ch 1, working in **back lps** *(see Stitch Guide)*, sc in each sc across, turn.

Rows 3–72: Rep row 2.

Row 73: Fold piece so starting ch is behind row 72, working in back lps of sc on row 72 and in corresponding unused lps of starting ch at same time, sl st in each sc across, turn piece so long edge is at top.

Crown
Rnd 1 (RS): Ch 1, now working in rounds around ends of rows, sc in each row around, **join** *(see Pattern Notes)* in beg sc. *(72 sc)*

Rnd 2: Ch 1, dc in same sc as joining, dc in each rem sc around, bring yarn to front, insert hook in first dc, yo with soft navy, draw lp through, turn.

Rnd 3: Ch 1, sl st in first dc, dc in next sc, *sl st in next dc, dc in next dc, rep from * around, insert hook in first sl st, yo with country blue, draw lp through, turn. Fasten off soft navy.

Rnd 4: Ch 1, dc in first st, dc in each rem dc and in each sl st around, bring yarn to front, insert hook in first dc, yo with white, draw lp through, turn.

Rnd 5: Ch 1, sl st in first dc, dc in next sc, *sl st in next dc, dc in next dc, rep from * around, insert hook in first sl st, yo with country blue, draw lp through, turn. Fasten off white.

Rnds 6–8: Rep rnds 2–4.

Rnd 9: Ch 1, sl st in first dc, dc in next sc, *sl st in next dc, dc in next dc, rep from * around, insert hook in first sl st, yo with country blue, draw lp through, turn. Fasten off white.

Continued on page 34

23

Man's Lapghan

Design by *Nazanin Fard*

Finished Size
44 inches x 55 inches,
excluding fringe

Materials
• Red Heart Super Saver
medium (worsted) weight
yarn (16 oz/835 yds/
438g per skein)
   3 skeins #0631
    light sage
• Size I/9/5.5mm crochet
hook or size needed to
obtain gauge
• Tapestry needle

Gauge
In pattern: 12 sts = 4 inches

Pattern Notes
Weave in ends as work progresses.

Chain-3 at beginning of row or round counts as first double crochet unless otherwise stated.

Afghan
Row 1 (WS): Ch 154, sc in 2nd ch from hook, sc each rem ch across, turn. *(153 sc)*

Row 2 (RS): Ch 3 *(see Pattern Notes)*, sk next 2 sc, tr in next sc, working behind tr just made, dc in each sk sc, dc in next sc, sk next sc, dc in each of next 2 sc, working in front of 2 dc just made, tr in sk sc, dc in next sc, rep from * across, turn.

Row 3: Ch 1, sc in each st across to beg ch-3, sc in 3rd ch of beg ch-3, turn.

Rep rows 2 and 3 alternately until piece measures 55 inches from beg, ending with a WS row. At end of last row, fasten off.

Side Edging
Row 1 (RS): Hold piece with RS facing and 1 long side at top, join yarn in end of first row in upper right-hand corner, ch 1, sc in same sp, *2 sc in end of next row, sc in end of next row, rep from * across. **Do not turn.**

Continued on page 35

Rasta Hat

Design by *Erica Taylor*

Skill Level

EASY

Finished Size
One size fits most

Materials
• Caron Simply Soft
Shadows medium
(worsted) weight yarn
(3 oz/150 yds/85g
per skein):
   1 skein #0001
   pearl frost
• Caron Simply Soft
medium (worsted) weight
yarn (6 oz/315 yds/170g
per skein):
   1 skein #9750 chocolate
• Size H/8/5mm crochet
hook or size needed to
obtain gauge
• Tapestry needle

Gauge
Rnds 1–3 = 4 inches

Pattern Notes
Weave in ends as work progresses.

Join with slip stitch as indicated unless otherwise stated.

Chain-3 at beginning of row or round counts as first double crochet unless otherwise stated.

Hat
Rnd 1 (RS): With pearl frost, ch 4, 14 dc in 4th ch from hook *(beg 3 chs count as a dc)*, **join** *(see Pattern Notes)* in 3rd ch of beg 3 sk chs. *(15 dc)*

Rnd 2: Ch 3 *(see Pattern Notes)*, dc in same ch as joining, 2 dc in each dc around, join in 3rd ch of beg ch-3. *(30 dc)*

Rnd 3: Rep rnd 2. *(60 dc at end of rnd)*

Rnd 4: Ch 3, dc in same ch as joining, dc in each of next 3 dc, *2 dc in next dc, dc in each of next 3 dc, rep from * around, join in 3rd ch of beg ch-3. *(75 dc)*

Rnd 5: Ch 3, dc in each dc around, join in 3rd ch of beg ch-3. Fasten off.

Rnd 6: Join chocolate in same ch as joining, ch 3, dc in same ch, dc in each of next 4 dc, *2 dc in next dc, dc in each of next 4 dc, rep from * around, join in 3rd ch of beg ch-3. *(90 dc)*

Rnd 7: Ch 3, dc in same ch as joining, dc in each of next 5 dc, *2 dc in next dc, dc in each of next 5 dc, rep from * around, join in 3rd ch of beg ch-3. *(105 dc)*

Rnd 8: Ch 3, dc in same ch as joining, dc in each of next 6 dc, *2 dc in next dc, dc in each of next 6 dc, rep from * around, join in 3rd ch of beg ch-3. Fasten off. *(120 dc)*

Rnd 9: Join pearl frost in same ch as joining, ch 3, dc in each dc around, join in 3rd ch of beg ch-3.

Rnd 10: Ch 3, dc in each dc around, join in 3rd ch of beg ch-3. Fasten off.

Rnd 11: Join chocolate in same ch as joining, ch 3, **dc dec** *(see Stitch Guide)* in next 2 dc, *dc in each of next 13 dc, dc dec in next 2 dc, rep from * 6 times, dc in each of last 12 dc, join in 3rd ch of beg ch-3. *(112 dc)*

Rnd 12: Ch 3, dc dec in next 2 dc, *dc in each of next 12 dc, dc dec in next 2 dc, rep from * 6 times, dc in each of last 11 dc, join in 3rd ch of beg ch-3. *(104 dc)*

Rnd 13: Ch 3, dc dec in next 2 dc, *dc in each of next 11 dc, dc dec in next 2 dc, rep from * 6 times, dc in each of last 10 dc, join in 3rd ch of beg ch-3. Fasten off. *(96 dc)*

Rnd 14: Join pearl frost in same ch as joining, ch 3, dc dec in next 2 dc, *dc in each of next 10 dc, dc dec in next 2 dc, rep from

* 6 times, dc in each of last 9 dc, join in 3rd ch of beg ch-3. *(88 dc)*

Rnd 15: Ch 3, dc dec in next 2 dc, *dc in each of next 9 dc, dc dec in next 2 dc, rep from * 6 times, dc in each of last 8 dc, join in 3rd ch of beg ch-3. *(80 dc)*

Rnd 16: Ch 3, dc dec in next 2 dc, *dc in each of next 8 dc, dc dec in next 2 dc, rep from * 6 times, dc in each of last 7 dc, join in 3rd ch of beg ch-3. Fasten off. *(72 dc)*

Rnd 17: Join chocolate in same ch as joining, ch 3, dc dec in next 2 dc, *dc in each of next 7 dc, dc dec in next 2 dc, rep from * 6 times, dc in each of last 6 dc, join in 3rd ch of beg ch-3. *(64 dc)*

Continued on page 35

Man's Black Hat

Design by *Diane Simpson*

Finished Size
23 inches in
circumference

Materials
• Patons Shetland
Chunky Tweeds bulky
(chunky) weight yarn
(3 oz/ 123 yds/85g
per ball):
    2 balls #67042
        charcoal tweed
• Size M/13/9mm crochet
hook or size needed to
obtain gauge
• Tapestry needle

Gauge
8 sc = 4 inches;
9 sc rnds =
4 inches

Pattern Notes
Weave in ends as
work progresses.

Join with
slip stitch as
indicated unless
otherwise stated.

Hat
Note: *Hat is*
worked in
continuous rounds.
Do not join unless
specified; mark beginning of rounds.

Rnd 1 (RS): Beg at top, ch 23, sc in 2nd ch from hook, sc in each
rem ch across, working in unused lps on opposite side of
starting ch, sc in each lp across. *(44 sc)*

Rnd 2: Sc in each sc around.

Rnds 3–17: Rep rnd 2. At end of last rnd, **join** *(see Pattern Notes)*
in next sc. Fasten off.

Rnd 18: Hold piece with RS facing, sk first sc from joining of previous rnd, join in next sc, turn, sc in sk sc, sc in next sl st, sc in each rem sc around.

Rnds 19–29: Rep rnd 2. At end of last rnd, join in next sc. Fasten off.

Finishing

Fold rnds 18–29 up twice to form brim. ●

Pop Top Mittens

Continued from page 11

Thumb

Rnd 1 (RS): Join yarn in first sk sc on rnd 15, ch 1, sc in same sc, sc in each rem sc, sc in next ch-1 sp, join in beg sc. *(16 sc)*

Rnd 2: Ch 1, sc in each sc around, join in beg sc.

Rnds 3–8: Rep rnd 2.

Rnd 9: Ch 1, **sc dec** *(see Stitch Guide)* in first 2 sc, [sc dec in next 2 sc] 7 times, join in beg sc. *(8 sc)*

Rnd 10: Rep rnd 2.

Rnd 11: Ch 1, sc dec in first 2 sc, [sc dec in next 2 sc] 3 times, join in beg sc. *(4 sc)*

Rnd 12: Rep rnd 2. Fasten off, leaving long end.

With tapestry needle, weave end through rem sc to close rnd securely.

Top

Rnd 1: Ch 4, join in first ch to form a ring, 6 sc in ring, join in beg sc. *(6 sc)*

Rnd 2: Ch 1, 2 sc in each sc around, join in beg sc. *(12 sc)*

Rnd 3: Ch 1, 2 sc in first sc, sc in next sc, [2 sc in next sc, sc in next sc] 5 times, join in beg sc. *(18 sc)*

Rnd 4: Ch 1, 2 sc in first sc, sc in each of next 2 sc, [2 sc in next sc, sc in each of next 2 sc] 5 times, join in beg sc. *(24 sc)*

Rnd 5: Ch 1, 2 sc in first sc, sc in each of next 3 sc, [2 sc in next sc, sc in each of next 3 sc] 5 times, join in beg sc. *(30 sc)*

Rnd 6: Ch 1, 2 sc in first sc, sc in each of next 4 sc, [2 sc in next sc, sc in each of next 4 sc] 5 times, join in beg sc. *(36 sc)*

Rnd 7: Ch 1, 2 sc in first sc, sc in each of next 5 sc, [2 sc in next sc, sc in each of next 5 sc] 5 times, join in beg sc. *(42 sc)*

Rnd 8: Ch 1, sc in each sc around, join in beg sc.

Rnds 9–21: Rep rnd 8. At end of last rnd, fasten off, leaving a 12-inch end for sewing.

Finishing

Sew bottom edge of Top to Hand, about 1 inch down from top edge. Sew halfway around, leaving palm open. Repeat on 2nd Mitten, making sure to reverse position of opening so palm is open on other hand. ●

Man's Hat & Scarf
Continued from page 13

Rnd 24: Ch 2, hdc in each st around, join in 2nd ch of beg ch-2. Fasten off.

Man's Scarf
Gauge
14 sts = 4 inches; 13 rows = 4 inches

Pattern Notes
Weave in ends as work progresses.

Chain-2 at beginning of row or round counts as first half double crochet unless otherwise stated.

Chain-3 at beginning of row or round counts as first double crochet unless otherwise stated.

Scarf
Note: Scarf is worked from side to side.
Row 1 (RS): With toast, ch 226, sc in 2nd ch from hook, sc in each rem ch across, turn. *(225 sc)*

Row 2: Ch 3 *(see Pattern Notes)*, dc in each sc across, **change color** *(see Stitch Guide)* to black in last dc, turn.

Row 3: Ch 1, sc in first dc, *fpdc *(see Stitch Guide)* loosely around next sc on 2 rows below, sc in each of next 5 dc, rep from * to last 3 sts, fpdc around next sc on 2nd row below, sc in next dc, sc in 3rd ch of beg ch-3, turn.

Row 4: Rep row 2, changing color to toast in last dc.

Row 5: Ch 1, sc in first dc, *fpdc around next fpdc on 2nd row below, sc in each of next 5 sc, rep from * to last 3 sts, fpdc around next fpdc on 2nd row below, sc in next dc, sc in 3rd ch of beg ch-3, turn.

Row 6: Rep row 2.

Row 7: Rep row 5.

Row 8: Rep row 2, changing to toast in last dc.

Row 9–16: [Rep rows 5–8 consecutively] twice.

Row 17: Ch 3, dc in each sc across, turn.

Row 18: Ch 2 *(see Pattern Notes)*, hdc in each dc across, turn.

Row 19: Ch 1, sl st in each hdc across. Fasten off.

Camo Hat & Scarf
Continued from page 16

Rnd 9: *Sc in next dc, dc in next sc, rep from * around.

Rnd 10: *Dc in next sc, sc in next dc, rep from * around.

Rnds 11–24: [Rep rnds 9 and 10 alternately] 7 times. At end of last rnd, join with sl st in first dc. Fasten off.

Brim

Row 1: Ch 10, sc in 2nd ch from hook, sc in each rem ch across, turn. *(9 sc)*

Row 2: Ch 1, working in **back lps** *(see Stitch Guide)* sc in each sc across, turn.

Rows 3–60: Rep row 2. At end of last row, fasten off.

Assembly

With tapestry needle, sew last row of Brim to edge of starting ch. Having seam at center back, sew 1 long edge of Brim to last rnd of Hat.

Side Edging

Hold piece with RS facing and 1 short end at top, join toast with sl st in end of first row in upper right-hand corner, work 22 sc evenly spaced across side. Fasten off. Rep on 2nd short side. ●

Man's Camo Scarf
Gauge

13 sc = 4 inches; 18 sc rows = 4 inches

Pattern Note

Weave in ends as work progresses.

Scarf

Row 1 (RS): Ch 215, sc in 2nd ch from hook, sc in each rem ch across, turn. *(214 sc)*

Row 2: Ch 1, working in **back lps** *(see Stitch Guide)*, sc in each sc across, turn.

Rows 3–20: Rep row 2.

Border

Working through both lps, sc in each sc across to next corner, ch 2, working across next side in ends of rows, work 12 sc evenly sp across to next corner, ch 2, working across next side in unused lps of starting ch, sc in each lp across, ch 2, working across next side in ends of rows, work 12 sc evenly sp across to next corner, ch 2, join with sl st in beg sc. Fasten off. ●

Travel Pillows
Continued from page 19

Row 2: Ch 1, sc in each sc across, turn.

Row 3: Ch 1, sc in each sc across. Fasten off.

Assembly

Hold pieces with RS together, with tapestry needle and Windsor blue, sew pieces together until there is an opening large enough to turn piece inside out and stuff. Turn inside out and stuff with fiberfill; then sew opening closed.

With tapestry needle and Windsor blue, sew Strap ends to each side of Row 1 of Front and Back.

Square Travel Pillow

Gauge

12 sc = 4 inches; 16 sc rows = 4 inches

Pattern Note

Weave in ends as work progresses.

Pillow

Front/Back

Make 1 of each color.

Row 1 (RS): Ch 41, sc in 2nd ch from hook, sc in each rem ch across, turn. *(40 sc)*

Row 2: Ch 1, sc in each sc across, turn. *(22 sc)*

Rows 3–35: Rep row 2. At end of last row, fasten off.

Strap

Row 1 (RS): With Windsor blue, ch 31, working in back bar of beg chs, sc in 2nd ch from hook, sc in each rem ch across, turn. *(30 sc)*

Row 2: Ch 1, sc in each sc across, turn.

Row 3: Ch 1, sc in each sc across. Fasten off.

Assembly

Hold pieces with RS together, with tapestry needle and Windsor blue, sew pieces together until there is an opening large enough to turn piece inside out and stuff. Turn piece right side out and stuff with fiberfill, then sew opening closed.

With tapestry needle and Windsor blue, sew Strap ends to each side of Row 1 of front and Back. ●

Camo Socks

Continued from page 21

Rnd 3: Ch 2, sc dec in next 2 sc, sc in each of next 19 sc, sc dec in next 2 sc, sc in each of next 16 sc, join in 2nd ch of beg ch-2, turn. (*38 sc*)

Rnd 4: Ch 2, sc dec in next 2 sc, sc in each of next 17 sc, sc dec in next 2 sc, sc in each of next 16 sc, join in 2nd ch of beg ch-2, turn. (*36 sc*)

Rnd 5: Ch 2, sc dec in next 2 sc, sc in each of next 15 sc, sc dec in next 2 sc, sc in each of next 16 sc, join in 2nd ch of beg ch-2, turn. (*34 sc*)

Rnd 6: Ch 2, sc dec in next 2 sc, sc in each of next 13 sc, sc dec in next 2 sc, sc in each of next 16 sc, join in 2nd ch of beg ch-2, turn. (*32 sc*)

Foot

Rnd 1 (RS): Ch 2, sc in each sc around, joining in 2nd ch of beg ch-2, turn.

Rnds 2–15 [2–16, 2–18]: Rep row 1. At end of last rnd, fasten off.

Toe

Rnd 1 (RS): Fold piece in half with Heel centered on bottom, place 2 markers 16 sts apart on right and left edge, join green at right-hand marker, ch 2, sc in each of next 13 sts, sc dec in next 2 sts, sc in each of next 14 sts, sc dec in last 2 sts, join in beg sc. (*30 sc*)

Rnd 2: Ch 2, sc in each of next 12 sc, sc dec in next 2 sc, sc in each of next 13 sc, sc dec in last 2 sts, join in beg sc, turn. (*28 sc*)

Rnd 3: Ch 2, sc in each of next 11 sc, sc dec in next 2 sc, sc in each of next 12 sc, sc dec in last 2 sts, join in beg sc, turn. (*26 sc*)

Rnd 4: Ch 2, sc in each of next 10 sc, sc dec in next 2 sc, sc in each of next 11 sc, sc dec in last 2 sts, join in beg sc, turn. (*24 sc*)

Rnd 5: Ch 2, sc in each of next 9 sc, sc dec in next 2 sc, sc in each of next 10 sc, sc dec in last 2 sts, join in beg sc, turn. (*22 sc*)

Rnd 6: Ch 2, sc in each of next 8 sc, sc dec in next 2 sc, sc in each of next 9 sc, sc dec in last 2 sts, join in beg sc, turn. (*20 sc*)

Rnd 7: Ch 2, sc in each of next 7 sc, sc dec in next 2 sc, sc in each of next 8 sc, sc dec in last 2 sts, join in beg sc, turn. (*18 sc*)

Rnd 8: Ch 2, sc in each of next 6 sc, sc dec in next 2 sc, sc in each of next 7 sc, sc dec in last 2 sts, join in beg sc. Fasten off. (*16 sc*)

Assembly

Turn Socks inside out. Fold Toes flat. Working through both thicknesses at same time, join camouflage in first sc, ch 2, sc in each sc across. Fasten off. ●

Blue/White Hat & Scarf
Continued from page 23

Rnd 10: Ch 1, dc in first st, dc in each of next 6 sts, **dc dec** (*see Stitch Guide*) in next 2 sts, *dc in each of next 7 sts, dc dec in next 2 sts, rep from * around, join in first dc, turn. (*64 dc*)

Rnd 11: Ch 1, dc dec in first 2 dc, *dc dec in next 2 dc, rep from * around, join in first dc, turn. (*32 dc*)

Rnd 12: Ch 1, dc in each of first 2 dc, dc dec in next 2 dc, *dc in each of next 2 dc, dc dec in next 2 dc, rep from * around, join in first dc, turn. (*24 dc*)

Rnd 13: Ch 1, dc dec in first 2 dc, *dc dec in next 2 dc, rep from * around, join in first dc. Leaving a 12-inch end for sewing, fasten off. (*12 dc*)

Finishing
With tapestry needle, weave end through last rnd. Gather tightly and sew to secure.

Blue/White Scarf
Gauge
7 sc = 2 inches

Pattern Notes
Weave in ends as work progresses.

Join with slip stitch as indicated unless otherwise stated.

Scarf

Row 1 (RS): With country blue, ch 25, sc in 2nd ch from hook, sc in each rem ch across, turn. (*24 sc*)

Row 2: Ch 1, sl st in first sc, dc in next sc, *sl st in next sc, dc in next sc, rep from * across, turn.

Row 3: Ch 1, dc in each st across. Fasten off.

Row 4: Hold piece with WS facing, **join** (*see Pattern Notes*) soft navy in first st, dc in next st, *sl st in next st, dc in next st, rep from * across. Fasten off.

Row 5: Hold piece with RS facing, join country blue in first st, ch 1, dc in same st, dc in each rem st across. Fasten off.

Row 6: Hold piece with WS facing, join white in first st, dc in next st, *sl st in next st, dc in next st, rep from * across. Fasten off.

Row 7: Rep row 5.

Rows 8–10: Rep rows 4–6.

Row 11: Hold piece with RS facing, join country blue in first st, ch 1, dc in same st, dc in each rem st across, turn.

Row 12: Ch 1, sl st in first st, dc in next st, *sl st in next st, dc in next st, rep from * across, turn.

Row 13: Ch 1, dc in each st across, turn.

Rows 14–107: [Rep rows 12 and 13 alternately] 47 times.

Row 108: Rep row 6.

Row 109: Rep row 5.

Rows 110 & 111: Rep rows 4 and 5.

Rows 112–114: Rep rows 108–110.

Rows 115 & 116: Rep rows 11 and 12.

Row 117: Ch 1, sc in each st across, turn.

Row 118: Ch 1, working in **back lps** (*see Stitch Guide*), sl st in each sc across. Fasten off. ●

Man's Lapghan
Continued from page 24

Row 2: Ch 1, working left to right, work **reverse sc** (*see Fig. 1*) in each sc across. Fasten off.

Rep on rem long side.

Fringe
Cut 10-inch strands of yarn. For each knot of fringe, fold 1 strand in half. From RS, draw folded end through first st on 1 short end. Draw ends through fold and tighten knot. Evenly space knots across both short ends. Trim ends evenly. ●

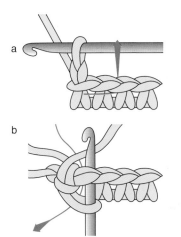
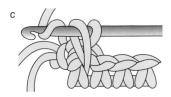

Fig 1.
Reverse Single Crochet

Rasta Hat
Continued from page 27

Rnd 18: Ch 3, dc in same ch as joining, *dc in each of next 4 dc, dc dec in next 2 dc, rep from * 9 times, dc in each of last 3 dc, join in 3rd ch of beg ch-3. (*55 dc*)

Rnd 19: Ch 2, hdc in same ch as joining, hdc in each st around, join in beg hdc. Fasten off. ●

Just for Women

Pamper yourself with these easy crochet projects that are classy, comfortable, cute and just for women.

Quick as a Wink Jacket

Design by *Darla Sims*

Gauge

With size K hook: 8 sts = 4 inches

Pattern Notes

Weave in ends as work progresses.

Chain-2 at beginning of row or round counts as first half double crochet unless otherwise stated.

Chain-3 at beginning of row or round counts as first half double crochet and chain-1 space unless otherwise stated.

Jacket

Back

Row 1 (RS): With size K hook, ch 39 [43, 47], sc in 2nd ch from hook, dc in next ch, *sc in next ch, dc in next ch, rep from * across, turn. *(38 [42, 46] sts)*

Row 2: Ch 1, sc in first dc, dc in next sc, *sc in next dc, dc in next sc, rep from * across, turn.

Rep row 2 until piece measures 13 inches from beg, ending with a WS row. Fasten off.

Front

Make 2.

Row 1 (RS): With size K hook, ch 21 [23, 25], sc in 2nd ch from hook, dc in next ch, *sc in next ch, dc in next ch, rep from * across, turn. *(20 [22, 24] sts)*

Continued on page 63

Skill Level
■■□□
EASY

Finished Sizes
Instructions given fit 32–34-inch bust *(small)*; changes for 36–38-inch *(medium)*, 40–42-inch bust *(large)* are in [ ].

Finished Garment Measurements
Bust: 38 inches *(small)* [42 inches *(medium)*, 44 inches *(large)*]

Materials
• Caron One Pound Rainbow Tones medium (worsted) weight yarn (10 oz/507 yds/284g per skein):
  2 [2, 3] skeins #602 denim tones
• Size J/10/6mm and K/10½/6.5mm crochet hooks or sizes needed to obtain gauge
• Tapestry needle
• Sewing needle
• 1¼-inch wooden buttons: 1
• Stitch markers
• Matching sewing thread

1·2·3 Skein Crochet

Felted Purse

Design by Lori Zeller

Finished Size
12 inches x 10 inches, excluding handle before felting
9½ inches x 9 inches, excluding handle after felting

Materials
• Lion Brand Lion Wool medium (worsted) weight wool (3 oz/158 yds/85g per ball:
   2 balls #153 ebony
   1 ball each #147 purple and #110 cadet blue
• Size G/6/4mm crochet hook or size needed to obtain gauge
• Tapestry needle
• Sewing needle
• 1 size 3 snap
• 7 assorted ½-inch–¾-inch black buttons
• Matching sewing thread

Gauge
12 dc = 3 inches; 7 dc rnds = 3 inches

Pattern Notes
Weave in ends as work progresses.

Join with slip stitch as indicated unless otherwise stated.

Chain-3 at beginning of row or round counts as first double crochet unless otherwise stated.

Finished size may vary due to amount of felting done.

Special Stitch
Long double crochet (long dc): Yo, working over ch sp, insert hook in indicated st on rnd below, draw up lp even with working row, [yo, draw through 2 lps on hook] twice.

Purse
Bottom
Row 1 (RS): With ebony, ch 4, sc in 2nd ch from hook, sc in each rem ch across, turn. *(3 sc)*

Row 2: Ch 1, 2 sc in first sc, sc in next sc, 2 sc in last sc, turn. *(5 sc)*

Row 3: Ch 1, 2 sc in first sc, sc in each of next 3 sc, 2 sc in last sc, turn. *(7 sc)*

Row 4: Ch 1, sc in each sc across, turn.

Rows 5–45: Rep row 4.

Row 46: Ch 1, **sc dec** (*see Stitch Guide*) in first 2 sc, sc in each of next 3 sc, sc dec in last 2 sc, turn. (*5 sc*)

Row 47: Ch 1, sc dec in first 2 sc, sc in next sc, sc dec in last 2 sc, turn. (*3 sc*)

Row 48: Ch 1, sc in each sc across, turn.

Body

Rnd 1: Ch 1, working around edge of piece, work 100 sc evenly sp around, **join** (*see Pattern Notes*) in beg sc.

Rnd 2: Ch 3, working in **back lps** (*see Stitch Guide*), dc in each sc around, join in first dc.

Rnd 3: Ch 3, dc in each dc around, join in top of first dc.

Rnd 4: Rep rnd 3. Fasten off.

Rnd 5: Join purple in same dc as joining, ch 1, sc in same dc, ch 1, sk next dc, *sc in next dc, ch 1, sk next dc, rep from * around, join in beg sc. Fasten off.

Rnd 6: Join cadet blue in same sc as joining, ch 1, sc in same sc, **long dc** (*see Special Stitch*) over next ch-space into st on rnd below ch, *sc in next sc, long dc over next ch-space into st on rnd below ch around, join in beg sc.

Rnd 7: Ch 3, dc in each st around, join in 3rd ch of beg ch-3. Fasten off.

Rnd 8: Join purple in same ch as joining, ch 1, sc in same ch as joining, ch 1, sk next dc, *sc in next sc, ch 1, sk next dc, rep from * around, join in first sc. Fasten off.

Rnd 9: Join ebony in same sc as joining, ch 1, sc in same sc, long dc in next sk dc on rnd below ch, *sc in next sc, long dc in next sk dc on rnd below ch, rep from * around, join in beg sc.

Rnd 10: Ch 3, dc in each st around, join in 3rd ch of beg ch-3.

Rnds 11–21: Rep rnd 10. At end of last rnd, fasten off.

Rnds 22–26: Rep rnds 5–9.

Rnds 27–29: Rep rnd 10.

Rnd 30: Ch 1, sc in first st, hdc in next st, dc in each of next 8 sts, hdc in next st, sc in each of next 40 sts, hdc in next st, dc in each of next 8 sts, hdc in next st, sc in each of last 39 sts, join in beg sc. Fasten off.

Rnd 31: Join purple with sc in first hdc worked on rnd 30, hdc in next dc, dc in each of next 6 dc, hdc in next dc, sc in each of next 42 sts, hdc in next dc, dc in each of next 6 dc, hdc in next dc, sc in each of next 41 sts, join in beg sc. Fasten off.

Rnd 32: Join cadet blue with sc in same sc as joining, hdc in next dc, dc in each of next 6 dc, hdc in next dc, sc in each of next 42 sts, hdc in next dc, dc in each of next 6 dc, hdc in next dc, sc in each of next 41 sts, join in joining sc.

First Strap

Row 1: Sl st in next hdc, sl st in next dc, ch 1, sc in same dc, sc in next dc, leaving rem sts unworked, turn. *(2 sc)*

Row 2: Ch 1, sc in each sc, turn.

Rows 3–160: Rep row 2.

Row 161: Ch 1, sc in each sc. Fasten off, leaving long end for sewing.

2nd Strap

Row 1: Join ebony with sc in next dc on rnd 32 from First Strap, sc in next sc, turn. *(2 sc)*

Rows 2–161: Rep rows 2–161 of First Strap.

3rd Strap

Row 1: Join purple with sc in next dc on rnd 32 from First Strap, sc in next sc, turn. *(2 sc)*

Rows 2–161: Rep rows 2–161 of First Strap.

Flap

Row 1: With ebony, ch 10, sc in 2nd ch from hook, sc in each rem ch across, turn. *(9 sc)*

Row 2: Ch 1, 2 sc in first sc, sc in each of next 7 sc, 2 sc in last sc, turn. *(11 sc)*

Row 3: Ch 1, 2 sc in first sc, sc in each of next 9 sc, 2 sc in last sc, turn. *(13 sc)*

Row 4: Ch 1, sc in each sc across, turn.

Row 5: Ch 1, 2 sc in first sc, sc in each of next 11 sc, 2 sc in last sc, turn. *(15 sc)*

Rows 6–36: Rep row 4. At end of last row, fasten off.

Inner Flap

Rows 1–35: With purple, rep rows 1–35 of Flap.

Row 36: Ch 1, sc in each sc across, turn.

Flap Edging

Rnd 1: Hold Inner Flap behind Flap, ch 1, working through both thicknesses at same time, sc evenly sp around outer edge, join in beg sc. Fasten off.

Rnd 38: Join cadet blue with sc in same sc as joining, ch 1, sc in each sc around and working 2 sc at each corner to keep piece flat, join in beg sc. Fasten off, leaving long end for sewing.

Large Flower

Rnd 1: With purple, ch 4, join in first ch to form a ring, ch 1, 8 sc in ring, join in first sc. *(8 sc)*

Rnd 2: Ch 1, working in **front lps** *(see Stitch Guide)*, (sc, ch 3, sc) in first sc, ch 1, sk next sc, *(sc, ch 3, sc) in next sc, ch 1, sk next sc, rep from * twice, join in beg sc.

Rnd 3: Sl st in next ch-3 sp, ch 1, (sc, 4 dc, sc) in same sp, sl st in next ch-1 sp, *(sc, 4 dc, sc) in next ch-3 sp, sl st in next ch-1 sp, rep from * twice, join in beg sc. Fasten off.

Rnd 4: Join cadet blue with sc in **back lp** *(see Stitch Guide)* of any st on rnd 1, 2 sc in next st, [sc in next st, 2 sc in next st] 3 times, join in beg sc.

Rnd 5: Ch 1, (sc, ch 3, sc) in first sc, ch 1, sk next sc, *(sc, ch 3, sc) in next sc, ch 1, sk next sc, rep from * 4 times, join in beg sc.

Rnd 6: Sl st in first ch-3 sp, ch 1, (sc, 5 dc, sc) in same sp, sl st in next ch-1 sp, *(sc, 5 dc, sc) in next ch-3 sp, sl st in next ch-1 sp, rep from * 4 times, join in beg sc. Fasten off, leaving long end for sewing.

Medium Flower

Make 1 cadet blue and 1 purple.

Rnd 1: Ch 4, join in first ch to form a ring, ch 1, 10 sc in ring, join in beg sc. *(10 sc)*

Rnd 2: Ch 1, (sc, ch 3, sc) in first sc, ch 1, sk next sc, *(sc, ch 3, sc) in next sc, ch 1, sk next sc, rep from * 3 times, join in beg sc.

Rnd 3: Sl st in next ch-3 sp, ch 1, (sc, 4 dc, sc) in same sp, sl st in next ch-1 sp, *(sc, 4 dc, sc) in next ch-3 sp, sl st in next ch-1 sp, rep from * 3 times, join in beg sc. Fasten off, leaving long end for sewing.

Small Flower

Make 2 cadet blue and 2 purple.

Rnd 1: Ch 4, join in first ch to form a ring, ch 1, [sc in ring, ch 3] 5 times, join in beg sc.

Rnd 2: Sl st in next ch-3 sp, ch 1, (sc, 4 dc, sc) in same sp, sl st in next ch-1 sp, *(sc, 4 dc, sc) in next ch-3 sp, sl st in next ch-1 sp, rep from * 3 times, join in beg sc. Fasten off, leaving long end for sewing.

Assembly

Braid Straps together. Sew ends to opposite sides of Purse. Sew top side of Flap to back top edge of Purse, centering Flap. Sew 1 button to center of each Flower. Sew large Flower to bottom section of flap. Referring to photo for placement, sew remaining Flowers to front of Purse.

Felting

Wash Purse in hot water and machine dry on high heat. Repeat washing and drying if desired. Press flowers open if needed.

Finishing

Sew 1 piece of large snap fastener to underside of Flap and sew remaining piece to Purse opposite first piece. ●

Basketweave Eyeglass Case

Design by Susan Lowman

Finished Size
3¾ inches x 7½ inches

Materials
• Red Heart Luster Sheen fine (sport) weight yarn (4 oz/335 yds/113g per skein):
  1 skein each #0227 buttercup and #0001 white
• Size F/5/3.75mm crochet hook or size needed to obtain gauge
• Tapestry needle
• Sewing needle
• 4¾ x 16-inch piece of white or yellow lining fabric
• ⅞-inch decorative button
• Hook closure
• Matching sewing thread
• Straight pins
• Seam sealant (optional)

Gauge
16 sts = 3 inches; 12 rnds = 3 inches

Pattern Notes
Weave in ends as work progresses.

Join with slip stitch as indicated unless otherwise stated.

Chain-2 at beginning of row or round counts as first double crochet unless otherwise stated.

Case
Rnd 1 (RS): Starting at bottom with buttercup, ch 40, being careful not to twist ch, **join** (*see Pattern Notes*) in first ch to from a ring, ch 1, sc in each ch around, join in beg sc. (*40 sc*)

Rnd 2: Ch 2 (*see Pattern Notes*), dc in each rem sc around, join from back to front in beg ch-2 sp.

Rnd 3: Ch 2, **fpdc** (*see Stitch Guide*) around next st, **bpdc** (*see Stitch Guide*) around each of next 2 dc, *fpdc around each of next 2 dc, bpdc around each of next 2 dc, rep from * around, join from front to back in beg ch-2 sp.

Rnd 4: Ch 2, bpdc around next st, fpdc around each of next 2 sts, *bpdc around each of next 2 sts, fpdc around each of next 2 sts, rep from * around, join from back to front in beg ch-2 sp.

Rnds 5–26: [Rep rnds 3 and 4 alternately] 11 times.

Rnd 27: Rep rnd 3.

Flap

Row 1 (RS): Ch 2, bpdc around next st, fpdc around each of next 2 sts, [bpdc around each of next 2 sts, fpdc around each of next 2 sts] 4 times, leaving rem 20 sts unworked, turn. (*20 sts*)

Row 2: Ch 2, fpdc around next st, bpdc around each of next 2 sts, [fpdc around each of next 2 sts, bpdc around each of next 2 sts] 3 times, fpdc around each of next 2 sts, bpdc around next st, bpdc around beg ch-2, turn.

Row 3: Ch 2, bpdc around next st, fpdc around each of next 2 sts, [bpdc around next 2 sts, fpdc around next 2 sts] 3 times, bpdc around each of next 2 sts, fpdc around next st, fpdc around beg ch-2, turn.

Row 4: Ch 2, fpdc around next st, bpdc around each of next 2 sts, [fpdc around each of next 2 sts, bpdc around each of next 2 sts] 3 times, fpdc around each of next 2 sts, bpdc around next st, bpdc around beg ch-2, turn.

Row 5: Sk first st, sl st in next st, sl st from front to back around post of next st, ch 2, fpdc around next st, bpdc around each of next 2 sts, [fpdc around each of next 2 sts, bpdc around each of next 2 sts] 3 times, leaving rem sts unworked, turn. (*16 sts*)

Row 6: Ch 2, bpdc around next st, fpdc around each of next 2 sts, [bpdc around each of next 2 sts, fpdc around each of next 2 sts] twice, bpdc around each of next 2 sts, fpdc around next st, fpdc around beg ch-2, turn.

Row 7: Sk first st, sl st in next st, sl st from back to front around post of next st, ch 2, bpdc around next st, fpdc around each of next 2 sts, [bpdc around each of next 2 sts, fpdc around each of next 2 sts] twice, leaving rem sts unworked, turn. (*12 sts*)

Row 8: Ch 2, fpdc around next st, bpdc around each of next 2 sts, fpdc around each of next 2 sts, bpdc around each of next 2 sts, fpdc around each of next 2 sts, bpdc around next st, bpdc around beg ch-2, turn.

Continued on page 65

Felted Necklace

Design by *Nazanin Fard*

Gauge
Gauge is not important for this project.

Pattern Notes
Weave in ends as work progresses.

Chain-3 at beginning of row or round counts as first double crochet unless otherwise stated.

Special Stitch
Bead single crochet (bead sc): Slide bead close to work, holding it to back of work, insert hook in indicated st, yo, draw lp through, yo, draw through 2 lps on hook.

Necklace
Note: *String beads on yarn.*

Ch 122, sk next ch, sc in next ch, **bead sc** *(see Special Stitch)* in each of next 30 chs, [ch 11, sc in 2nd ch from hook, bead sc in each of next 9 chs of starting ch *(spoke)*, bead sc in each of next 3 chs] 19 times, ch 11, sc in 2nd ch from hook, bead sc in each of next 9 chs *(spoke)*, bead sc in each of next 30 chs. Fasten off. *(20 spokes)*

Felted Ball
Make 20.

Note: *Ball is worked in continuous rnds. Do not join unless specified; mark beg of rnds.*

Rnd 1 (RS): Make slip knot on hook, 5 sc in slip knot ring, pull end to tighten hole.

Rnd 2: Bead sc (*see Special Stitch*) in each of next 5 sc.

Rnd 3: Rep rnd 2.

Rnd 4: [Sk next sc, sc in next sc] twice, sk next sc.

Rnd 5: Sk next sc, sc in next sc. Fasten off.

Felting

Soak Necklace in lukewarm water for 15 minutes. Spread piece out on blocking board, pinning all Spokes out straight.
Let dry.

Place Balls in small pillowcase and place in washer with pair of jeans. Wash with hot water and rinse in cold water until Balls are felted desired amount.
Let dry.

Finishing

Sew 1 Ball to end of each Spoke. Sew clasp at beg of row 1. Sew hook to opposite end of same row. ●

Dainty Slippers

Design by *Shirley Patterson*

Sizes

Instructions given fit shoe size small/medium; changes for large/X-large are in [ ].

Finished Sizes

Foot length: 8½ inches *(small/medium)* [10 inches *(large/X-large)*].

Materials

• NaturallyCaron.com Country medium (worsted) weight yarn (3 oz/185 yds/ 85g per skein):
  2 (3) skeins
    #0010 sunset
• Size J/10/6mm crochet hook or size needed to obtain gauge
• Tapestry needle
• Sewing needle
• 2 metal ⅝-inch buttons
• Matching sewing thread

Gauge

With 2 strands held tog: 4 sc = 1 inch

Pattern Notes

Weave in ends as work progresses.

Join with slip stitch as indicated unless otherwise stated.

Chain-2 at beginning of row or round counts as first double crochet unless otherwise stated.

Special Stitch

Popcorn (pc): 3 dc in indicated st, drop lp from hook, insert hook in first dc made, draw lp through.

Slipper

Make 2.

Row 1 (WS): Starting at heel and leaving 40-inch end, ch 30, sc in 2nd ch from hook, sc in each of next 13 chs, sl st in next ch, sc in each of next 14 chs, turn. *(28 sc, 1 sl st)*

Row 2 (RS): Ch 4, dc in first st, ch 1, sk next st, [**pc** *(see Special Stitch)* in next st, ch 1, sk next st] 5 times, 2 pc in next st, ch 1, pc in next st, ch 1, sk next sl st, pc in next st, ch 1, 2 pc in next st, ch 1, sk next st, [pc in next st, ch 1, sk next st] 5 times, dc in last sc, turn. *(16 pc, 2 dc, 15 ch-1 sps)*

Row 3: Ch 1, sc in each st and in each ch-1 sp across, turn.

Row 4: Ch 4, dc in first sc, ch 1, sk next sc, [pc in next sc, ch 1, sk next sc] 15 times, dc in last sc, turn. *(15 pc, 2 dc, 16 ch-1 sps)*

Rows 5–8 [5–12]: [Rep rows 3 and 4 alternately] 2 [4] times.

Row 9 [13]: Ch 1, sc in each st and in each ch across, turn, sl st in each of first 5 sc *(mark first sl st made)*, ch 9, sl st in 5th sc from beg of same row, turn.

Rnd 10 [14]: Now working in rnds, ch 3, pc in first ch of next ch-9 [ch-11] sp, [ch 1, sk next ch, pc in next ch] 4 [5] times, ch 1, [pc in next sc, ch 1, sk next sc] 12 times, sk beg ch-3, **join** *(see Pattern Notes)* in first pc. *(17 [18] pc, 17 [18] ch-1 sps)*

Rnd 11 [15]: Ch 1, sc in each of first 10 [11] sc, **sc dec** *(see Stitch Guide)* in next 2 sc, sc in each of next 10 sc, sc dec in next 2 sc, sc in each of next 10 [11] sc. *(32 [34] sc)*

Rnd 12 [16]: Ch 3, *pc in next sc, ch 1, sk next sc, rep from * around, sk beg ch-3, join in first pc. *(16 [17] pc, 16 [17] sc)*

Rnd 13 [17]: Ch 1, sc in each of first 10 [11] sc, sc dec in next 2 sc, sc in each of next 8 sc, sc dec in next 2 sc, sc in each of next 10 [11] sc, join in beg sc. *(30 [32] sc)*

Rnd 14 [18]: Rep rnd 12. *(15 [16] pc, 15 [16] sc)*

Rnd 15 [19]: Ch 1, sc in each of first 9 [10] sc, sc dec in next 2 sc, sc in each of next 8 sc,

sc dec in next 2 sc, sc in each of next 9 [10] sc, join in beg sc. *(28 [30] sc)*

Rnd 16 [20]: Rep rnd 12. *(14 [15] pc, 14 [15] sc)*

Rnd 17 [21]: Ch 1, sc in each of first 8 [9] sc, sc dec in next 2 sc, sc in each of next 8 sc, sc dec in next 2 sc, sc in each of next 8 [9] sc, join in beg sc. *(26 [28] sc)*

Rnd 18 [22]: Rep rnd 12. *(13 [14] pc, 13 [14] sc)*

Rnd 19 [23]: Ch 1, [sc dec in next 3 sts] 8 times, [sc dec in next 2 sc] 1 [2] times, join in beg sc, ch 1, sl st in each of first 4 [5] sc, turn. *(9 [10] sc)*

Rnd 20 [24]: Flatten previous rnd, ch 1, working through both thicknesses, sc in each st around, join in first sl st made at end of previous rnd. Fasten off.

Continued on page 66

Updated Ruffled Scarf

Design by Jewdy Lambert

Skill Level

EXPERIENCED

Finished Size
2 inches x 144 inches

Materials
• Universal Yarn Tango medium (worsted) weight yarn (1¾ oz/23 yds/50g per skein):
   2 skeins #584 orange/red variegated
• Size D/3/3.25mm crochet hook
• Tapestry needle
• Sewing needle
• Matching sewing thread

Gauge
Gauge not important to this project.

Pattern Notes
The scarf is made using chain stitches only. Use crochet hook to take a bite (loop) of yarn every 1-inch along outer edge and pull a loop through on hook. The 1-inch gathers make scarf spiral by itself. One half of scarf is worked with one color on outer edge; other half of scarf is worked with opposite edge on border. The fullness of the ruffle is controlled by the distance between the first piercing and the next. It is recommended that these distances be ½ to 1 inch apart, although consistency in whatever length is more important.

Scarf
Row 1: Hold yarn in left hand. Leaving 1-inch end, insert hook just under woven edge of yarn, pull a small bite *(lp)* of yarn onto hook, *move hook forward about 1 inch, insert hook under woven edge again, pull another small bite *(lp)* through lp on hook *(ch st)*, rep from * until piece measures 36 inches, turn.

Row 2: Turn yarn over. Working in ch sts of row 1, insert hook in **back lp** *(see Stitch Guide)* of first st, *extend hook 1 inch through lp and move hook 1 inch farther along tape yarn, insert hook under edge, take a small bite *(lp)*, pull bite *(lp)* through 2 lps on hook, insert hook in back lp of next ch st,

rep from * across. To fasten off, remove lp from hook. Secure lp with sewing needle and matching sewing thread.

Rep rows 1 and 2 with 2nd skein, using opposite colored edge.

Finishing

Sew both pieces together at 1 short end. Sew under raw edges of yarn. ●

Hoodie Scarf

Design by *Glenda Winkleman*

Size
8 inches x 80 inches,
excluding Fringe

Materials
• Moda Dea Tweedle Dee
bulky (chunky) weight
yarn (3½ oz/155 yds/100g
per skein):
   3 skeins #8906
   cinnamon twist
• Size K/10½/6.5mm
crochet hook or size
needed to obtain gauge
• Tapestry needle

Gauge

(2 dc, ch 2, sc) = 3 inches; 9 rows = 6 inches

Pattern Notes

Weave in ends as work progresses.

Chain-3 at beginning of row or round counts as first double
crochet unless otherwise stated.

Scarf

Row 1 (RS): Ch 22, (dc, ch 2, dc) in 4th ch from hook, *sk next
2 chs, (2 dc, ch 2, sc) in next ch, rep from * across, turn.

Row 2: Sl st in next ch-2 sp, **ch 3** *(see Pattern Notes)*, (dc, ch 2, sc)
in same sp, (2 dc, ch 2, sc) in each rem ch-2 sp across, turn.

Rows 3–119: Rep row 2. At end of last row, fasten off.

Assembly

Fold piece in half with WS together. For hood, starting at
top center, sew through both thicknesses for 10 inches on
1 side only.

Hood Edging

Note: *Mark 15th row on each side from center row at top of hood.*
Row 1 (RS): Hold piece with RS facing and edge of hood at top,
join yarn in end of marked row on right-hand side of center, ch
3, (dc, ch 2, sc) in same sp, *sk next row, (2 dc, ch 2, sc) in next
row, rep from * 14 times, leaving rem rows unworked, turn.

Row 2: Sl st in next ch-2 sp, ch 3, (dc, ch 2, sc) in same sp, (2 dc, ch 2, sc) in each rem ch-2 sp across. Fasten off.

Fringe

Cut 42 pieces of yarn, each 11 inches long. For each knot of fringe, fold 3 strands in half. From RS, draw folded end through first ch-2 sp on 1 short end. Draw ends through fold and tighten knot. Place knots in rem ch-2 sps on both short ends. Trim ends even. ●

Angora Scarf & Gloves

Design by *Jewdy Lambert*

- -

Scarf
Gauge
8½ sc = 2 inches

Pattern Notes
Weave in ends as work progresses.

Join with slip stitch as indicated unless otherwise stated.

Chain-2 at beginning of row or round counts as first single crochet unless otherwise stated.

Chain-4 at beginning of row or round counts as first double crochet and chain-1 space unless otherwise stated.

Neck Scarf
Row 1 (RS): Ch 14, sc in 3rd ch from hook *(beg 2 sk chs count as a dc)*, sc in each rem ch across, turn. *(15 sc)*

Row 2: Ch 2 *(see Pattern Notes)*, sc in each of next 5 sc, ch 3, sk next 3 sc, sc in each of next 6 sc, turn.

Row 3: Ch 2, sc in each of next 5 sc, 3 sc in next ch-3 sp, sc in each of next 6 sc, turn.

Row 4: Ch 2, sc in each sc across, turn.

Rep row 4 until piece measures 20 inches from beg, ending with a WS row. At end of last row, fasten off.

Skill Level
■■□□
EASY

Finished Size
Scarf: 5 inches x 20½ inches
Gloves: One size fits most

Materials
Scarf
• Angora medium (worsted) weight yarn:
  1 oz/55 yds/28g lilac
  10 yds each purple and mauve
• Size G/6/4mm crochet hook or size needed to obtain gauge
• Tapestry needle
Gloves
• Angora medium (worsted) weight yarn:
  1 oz/55 yds/28g lilac
  10 yds each purple and mauve
• Size I/9/5.5mm crochet hook or size needed to obtain gauge
• Tapestry needle

Edging

Rnd 1 (RS): Hold piece with RS facing and last row at top, **join** (see Pattern Notes) purple in last sc of last row, ch 2, sc in same sc, working across next side in ends of rows, sc in each row, working across next side in unused lps of starting ch, 2 sc in first lp, sc in each rem lp across to last lp, 2 sc in last lp, working across next side in ends of rows, sc in each row across, working across last row, 2 sc in next sc, sc in each sc across to beg ch-2, join in 2nd ch of beg ch-2.

Row 2: Now working in a row, ch 2, *sk next 2 sc, 5 dc in next sc, sk next 2 sc, sc in next sc, rep from * around to last sc at end of 2nd long side. Leaving last short side unworked, fasten off.

Flower

Rnd 1 (RS): With mauve, ch 4, join in first ch to form a ring, **ch 4** (see Pattern Notes), [dc in ring, ch 1] 7 times, join in 3rd ch of beg ch-4. (8 dc, 8 ch-1 sps)

Rnd 2: Ch 2, 4 dc in next ch-1 sp, sc in next ch-1 sp, 4 dc in next ch-1 sp, rep from * around, join in 2nd ch of beg ch-2. Leaving 8-inch end for sewing, fasten off.

Leaf

Make 2.

With mauve, ch 15, sc in 2nd ch from hook, hdc in next ch, dc in each of next 2 chs, tr in each of next 4 chs, dc in each of next 3 chs, hdc in next ch, sc in next ch, working in opposite lps on opposite side of ch, hdc in next lp, dc in each of next 2 lps, tr in each of next 4 lps, dc in each of next 3 lps, hdc in next lp, sc in next lp. Leaving 8-inch end of sewing, fasten off.

Finishing

Referring to photo for placement, sew Flower to Scarf 1 inch from ch-3 sp on row 2. Sew Leaves to Scarf 2 inches from opposite end.

Gloves

Gauge

4 dc =1 inch

Pattern Notes

Weave in ends as work progresses.

Join with slip stitch as indicated unless otherwise stated.

Chain-3 at beginning of row or round counts as first double crochet unless otherwise stated.

Fingerless Glove

Make 2.

Row 1 (RS): With lilac, ch 18, dc in 4th ch from hook (beg 3 chs count as a dc), dc in each rem ch across, turn. (16 dc)

Row 2: Ch 3 (see Pattern Notes), working in **back lps** (see Stitch Guide), dc in each dc across, turn.

Rows 3–13: Rep row 2.

Row 14: Fold piece so starting ch is behind row 13, working through both thicknesses at same time, sl st in each of first 11 dc. Leaving rem sts unworked, fasten off.

Turn seam to WS.

Hand

Rnd 1 (RS): Hold Cuff with RS facing and 1 long edge at top, **join** (*see Pattern Notes*) lilac in seam, ch 3, work 35 dc evenly sp around edge, join in 3rd ch of beg ch-3, turn. *(36 dc)*

Rnd 2: Ch 3, dc in each dc around, join in 3rd ch of beg ch-3, turn.

Rnds 3–6: Rep rnd 2.

Rnd 7: Ch 3, dc in each of next 12 dc, sk next 10 dc (*thumb opening*), dc in each rem dc around, join in 3rd ch of beg ch-3, turn. *(25 dc)*

Rnds 8 & 9: Rep rnd 2. At end of last rnd, fasten off.

Edging

Join purple in same ch as joining of rnd 9, ch 1, sc in same ch, sc in each dc around, join in beg sc.

Thumb Opening Edging

Join purple in first sk dc on rnd 6, ch 1, sc in same dc, sc in each sk dc around, join in beg sc.

Flower

Rnd 1 (RS): With mauve, ch 4, join in first ch to form a ring, **ch 4** (*see Pattern Notes*), [dc in ring, ch 1] 7 times, join in 3rd ch of beg ch-4. *(8 dc, 8 ch-1 sps)*

Rnd 2: Ch 2, 4 dc in next ch-1 sp, sc in next ch-1 sp, 4 dc in next ch-1 sp, rep from * around, join in 2nd ch of beg ch-2. Leaving 8-inch end for sewing, fasten off.

Finishing

Referring to photo for placement, sew 1 Flower to each Glove. ●

Jewelry Roll

Design by *Brenda Stratton*

Finished Size
13 inches x 7 inches, unfolded

Materials
• Caron Simply Soft medium (worsted) weight yarn (6 oz/315 yds/ 170g per skein):
    1 skein #9705 sage
    1 oz/50 yds/28g #9702 off-white
• Size G/6/4mm crochet hook or size needed to obtain gauge
• Tapestry needle
• Straight pins

Gauge
5 sc = 1 inch; 5 sc rows = 1 inch

Pattern Notes
Weave in ends as work progresses unless otherwise specified.

Join with slip stitch as indicated unless otherwise stated.

Chain-3 at beginning of row or round counts as first double crochet unless otherwise stated.

Special Stitch
Surface slip stitch (surface sl st): Insert hook in indicated sp, yo, draw lp through from back to front, draw lp through lp on hook.

Jewelry Roll
Outer Section
Row 1 (RS): Starting at lower edge with sage, ch 31, sc in 2nd ch from hook, sc in each rem ch across, turn. *(30 sc)*

Row 2: Ch 1, sc in each st across, turn.

Rows 3–18: Rep row 2.

Row 19: Working in **front lps** (*see Stitch Guide*), sc in each sc across, turn.

Rows 20–40: Rep row 2.

Row 41: Rep row 19.

Rows 42–62: Rep row 2.

Row 63: Rep row 19.

Row 64: Ch 1, sc in each sc across. Fasten off.

Horizontal Trim

Hold piece with RS facing and off-white on WS of work, insert hook in sp between first 2 sc on row 21, yo, draw lp through, leaving an 8-inch end on WS, work **surface sl st** (*see Special Stitch*) in next sp between sc on same row, work surface sl st in each rem sp between sc across row. Drop lp from hook. Cut yarn, leaving an 8-inch end.

Note: *Do not weave in ends until indicated.* Working in sps between sc of row 42, rep Horizontal Trim.

Pocket
Make 3.

Row 1 (WS): Starting at lower edge with sage, ch 31, sc in 2nd ch from hook, sc in each rem ch across, turn. (*30 sc*)

Row 2: Ch 1, sc in each sc across, turn.

Rows 3–17: Rep row 2. At end of last row, fasten off.

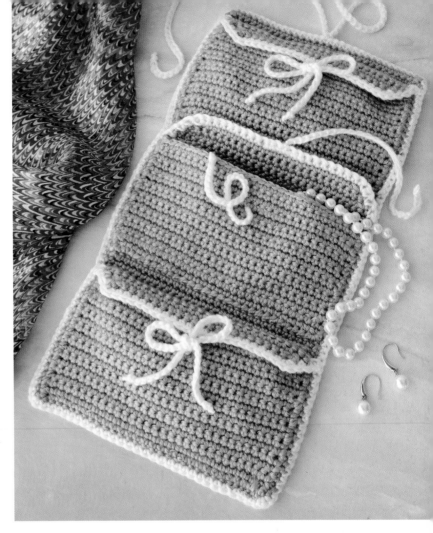

Pocket and Outer Shell Assembly

On WS, place lower edge of 1 Pocket on upper Horizontal Trim. With tapestry needle and sage, sew lower edge of Pocket to Horizontal Trim. Pin sides to Outer Section with top of Pocket 1 row below unused lps of row 62.

Place lower edge of 2nd Pocket on remaining Horizontal Trim. Sew lower edge of Pocket to Horizontal Trim. Pin sides to Outer Section with top of Pocket 1 row below unused lps of row 40.

Place lower edge of 3rd Pocket on lower edge of Outer Section, pin in place. Pin sides to Outer Section with top of Pocket 1 row below unused lps of row 18.

Continued on page 66

Size
Hat: One size fits most
Scarf: 6 inches x 60 inches, including ruffle trim

Materials
Hat
• Henry's Attic Island Cotton bulky (chunky) weight yarn (8 oz/370 yds/226g per skein):
   2 skeins natural
• Universal Yarn Tango medium (worsted) weight yarn (1¾ oz/23 yds/50g per skein):
   1 skein #587 purple/ turquoise/camel variegated
• Sizes D/3/3.25mm and I/9/5.5mm crochet hooks or sizes needed to obtain gauge
• Tapestry needle
• Sewing needle
• Matching sewing thread
Scarf
• Henry's Attic Island Cotton bulky (chunky) weight yarn (8 oz/370 yds/ 226g per skein):
   2 skeins natural
• Universal Yarn Tango medium (worsted) weight yarn (1¾ oz/23 yds/50g per skein:
   1 skein #587 purple/ turquoise/camel variegated
• Sizes D/3/3.25mm and I/9/5.5mm crochet hooks or sizes needed to obtain gauge
• Tapestry needle
• Sewing needle
• Matching sewing thread

Ruffle Trim Hat & Scarf

Design by *Jewdy Lambert*

• •

Hat
Gauge
Rnds 1–3 = 2½ inches

Pattern Notes
Weave in ends as work progresses.

Join with slip stitch as indicated unless otherwise stated.

Chain-2 at beginning of row or round counts as first single crochet unless otherwise stated.

Hat
Rnd 1 (RS): With size I hook and natural, ch 4, **join** (*see Pattern Notes*) in first ch to form a ring, **ch 2** (*see Pattern Notes*), 7 sc in ring, join in 2nd ch of beg ch-2. (*8 sc*)

Rnd 2: Ch 2, sc in same ch as joining, 2 sc in each sc around, join in 2nd ch of beg ch-2. (*16 sc*)

Rnd 3: Ch 2, sc in each sc around, join in 2nd ch of beg ch-2.

Rnd 4: Ch 2, sc in same ch as joining, 2 sc in each sc around, join in 2nd ch of beg ch-2. (*32 sc*)

Rnd 5: Rep rnd 3.

Rnd 6: Ch 2, sc in next sc, *2 sc in next sc, sc in each of next 2 sc, rep from * around, join in 2nd ch of beg ch-2. (*42 sc*)

Rnds 7 & 8: Rep rnd 3.

Rnd 9: Ch 2, sc in next sc, *2 sc in next sc, sc in each of next 2 sc, rep from * around, join in 2nd ch of beg ch-2. *(56 sc)*

Rnds 10–21: Rep rnd 3. At end of last rnd, fasten off.

Flower

Make 3.

With size D hook and holding variegated in left hand, insert hook just under woven edge, gather 1-inch section of yarn on hook, *push hook forward about 1 inch and move forward same distance along yarn, insert hook under woven edge again and draw through lp on hook, rep from * until piece measures 12 inches. To fasten off, remove lp from hook. Secure lp with sewing needle and matching sewing thread.

Finishing

Tighten each Flower into a rose shape. With sewing needle and matching sewing thread, sew under raw edges of variegated. Referring to photo for placement, sew Flowers to Hat.

Scarf

Gauge

Gauge not important to this project.

Pattern Notes

Weave in ends as work progresses.

Join with slip stitch as indicated unless otherwise stated.

Chain-3 at beginning of row or round counts as first double crochet unless otherwise stated.

Scarf

Row 1 (RS): With size I hook and natural, ch 20, dc in 4th ch from hook *(beg 3 sk chs count as a dc)*, dc in each rem ch across, turn. *(18 dc)*

Row 2: Ch 3 *(see Pattern Notes)*, dc in each dc across, turn.

Rows 3–77: Rep row 2. At end of last row, fasten off.

Flower

Make 3.

With size D hook and holding variegated in left hand, insert hook just under woven edge, gather 1-inch section of yarn on hook, *push hook forward about 1 inch and move forward same distance along yarn, insert hook under woven edge again and draw through lp on hook, rep from * until piece measures 12 inches. To fasten off, remove lp from hook. Secure lp with sewing needle and matching sewing thread.

Ruffle

With size D hook and holding variegated yarn in left hand, insert hook just under woven edge and take a bite *(lp)* of fabric on hook. Leaving lp on hook, push crochet hook forward about 1 inch, insert hook under woven edge again, take another bite *(lp)* and pull back through lp on hook.

Starting at base of 2nd row of Scarf, with gathered st still on hook, *take a bite of Scarf, then 2 bites of gathered sts, rep from * across row, turn Scarf over and working in top of row 1, work in same manner across row, turn Scarf over and work across base of row 1 in same manner. To fasten off, remove lp from hook. Secure lp with sewing needle and matching sewing thread. Sew raw edges of variegated. Rep on opposite end of Scarf.

Finishing

Tighten each Flower into a rose shape. With sewing needle and matching sewing thread, sew under raw edges of variegated. Referring to photo for placement, sew approximately 9¼ inches from 1 end of Scarf. ●

Quick as a Wink Jacket

Continued from page 39

Row 2: Ch 1, sc in first dc, dc in next sc, *sc in next dc, dc in next sc, rep from * across, turn.

Rep row 2 until piece measures 13 inches from beg, ending with a WS row. Fasten off.

Sleeve

Make 2.

Row 1 (RS): With size K hook, ch 31 [33, 35], sc in 2nd ch from hook, dc in next ch, *sc in next ch, dc in next ch, rep from * across, turn. *(30 [32, 34] sts)*

Row 2: Ch 1, sc in first dc, dc in next sc, *sc in next dc, dc in next sc, rep from * across, turn.

Rep row 2 until piece measures 14 inches from beg, ending with a WS row. Fasten off.

Yoke

Row 1 (RS): Hold 1 Front with RS facing, with size K hook, join yarn with sc in first dc, dc in next sc, *sc in next dc, dc in next sc, rep from * across, hold 1 Sleeve with RS facing, sc in first dc on Sleeve, dc in next sc, **sc in next dc, dc in next sc, rep from ** across, hold Back with RS facing, sc in first dc on Back, dc in next sc, ***sc in next dc, dc in next sc, rep from *** across, hold rem Sleeve with RS facing, sc in first dc on Sleeve, dc in next sc, ****sc in next dc, dc in next sc, rep from **** across, hold rem Front with RS facing, sc in first dc on Front, dc in next sc, *****sc in next dc, dc in next sc, rep from ***** across, turn. *(138 [150, 162] sts)*

Row 2: Ch 1, sc in first dc, dc in next sc, *sc in next dc, dc in next sc, rep from * across, turn.

Rep row 2 until Yoke measures 4 [4½, 5] inches from beg, ending with a WS row.

Upper Yoke

Row 1: Ch 1, sc in first dc, **sc dec** *(see Stitch Guide)* in next 2 sts, sc in next st, rep from * across to last 2 sts, sc dec in last 2 sts, turn. *(92 [100, 108] sc)*

Row 2: With size J hook, **ch 3** *(see Pattern Notes)*, dc in each sc across, turn.

Row 3: Ch 1, sc in first dc, *sc dec in next 2 dc, sc in next dc, rep from * across to last 4 [3, 2] dc, sc dec in next 2 dc, sc in each of next 2 [1, 0] dc, turn. *(62 [67, 71] sc)*

Row 4: Ch 3, dc in each sc across, turn.

Row 5: Ch 1, sc in each dc across, turn.

Row 6: Ch 3, dc in each sc across, turn.

Row 7: Ch 1, sc in first dc, *sc dec in next 2 dc, sc in next dc, rep from * across to last 4 [3, 2] dc, sc dec in next 2 dc, sc in each of next 2 [1, 0] dc. Fasten off. *(42 [45, 48] sc)*

Assembly

Sew Sleeve and side seams in 1 continuous seam.

Edging

Rnd 1 (RS): Hold piece with RS facing and starting ch at top, with size J hook, join yarn with sc in right side seam, working in unused lps of starting ch, sc in each lp across to next corner, 3 sc in corner, working across right front edge in ends of rows, work 40 [42, 44] sc evenly sp to next corner, 3 sc in corner, working around neck edge, sc in each sc to next corner, 3 sc in corner, working across left front edge in ends of rows, work 40 [42, 44] sc evenly sp to next corner, 3 sc in corner, working across next side in unused lps of starting ch, sc in each lp to beg sc, join in joining sc.

Note: Place marker for button on Left Front. Place marker on Right Front opposite first marker for button lp.

Rnd 2: Ch 1, sc in each st to 2nd sc of next corner, 3 sc in 2nd sc, sc in each sc to marker, ch 4 *(or number of chs needed to fit snuggly around button)*, sk next 4 sc *(or same number of sts as needed for button lp)*, sc in each sc to 2nd sc of next corner, 3 sc in 2nd sc, sc in each sc to 2nd sc of next corner, 3 sc in 2nd sc, sc in each sc to 2nd sc of next corner, 3 sc in 2nd sc, sc in each sc to beg sc join in beg sc. Fasten off.

Finishing

Sew button opposite button loop. ●

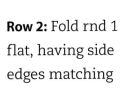

Basketweave Eyeglass Case
Continued from page 45

Row 9: Sk first st, sl st in next st, sl st from front to back around post of next st, ch 2, fpdc around next st, bpdc around each of next 2 sts, fpdc around each of next 2 sts, bpdc around each of next 2 sts, leaving rem sts unworked, turn. *(8 sts)*

Row 10: Ch 2, bpdc around next st, fpdc around each of next 2 sts, bpdc around each of next 2 sts, fpdc around next st, fpdc around beg ch-2. Fasten off.

Top Edging

Hold piece with RS facing, join white in joining sl st at end of rnd 27, working across side of Flap in ends of rows and in unused sts of even-number rows, sc evenly sp to row 10, working across row 10, 2 sc in first st, sc in each st to last st, 2 sc in last st, working across next side of Flap in ends of rows and in unused sts of even-number rows, sc evenly sp to row 1 of Flap, working in rem unused sc on rnd 27 of Case, sc in each sc around, join in beg sl st. Fasten off.

Lower Edging

Rnd 1 (RS): Hold Case with RS facing and starting ch at top, working in unused lps of starting ch, join buttercup with sc in first lp, sc in each rem lp around, join in beg sc. Fasten off. *(40 sc)*

Row 2: Fold rnd 1 flat, having side edges matching edges of Flap, now working in a row and working over sc on rnd 1 into same unused lps of starting ch as sc made, join white in first unused lp at right-hand edge, sc in each rem unused lp across. Fasten off.

Lining

With RS together, fold fabric in half lengthwise to form 4¾ x 8-inch piece. Sew seam along both 8-inch edges, having ½-inch seam allowance. Zigzag-stitch edges or apply Stop Fraying to all raw edges (if needed) and allow to dry. Insert piece into Case. Fold top edge of fabric down to WS about 1 inch or as needed and pin. Remove Lining and sew folded edge ½ inch from edge. Insert Lining back into Case and sew top edge of Lining to top edge of Case below Flap, matching side seams of Lining with edges of Case.

Finishing

Referring to photo for placement, sew decorative button to front of Flap. Sew hook closure to back of Flap behind button and to front of eyeglass case in corresponding place. ●

Dainty Slippers
Continued from page 49

Assembly

Hold piece with RS facing and heel at top, fold piece in half with WS tog, with ends left at beg of starting ch and working through both thicknesses at same time, sl st across edge. Fasten off.

Edging

Hold piece with RS facing, join 2 strands of yarn in marked sl st on rnd 9 [13], ch 1, (sc, ch 3, sc) in same st as joining *(button lp)*, sc in each of next 2 sl st, sc dec in next sl and in ch at base of next pc, sc in each ch across to ch at base of last pc, sc dec in ch at base of last pc and in next sc, sc in each of next 2 sts, (sc, ch 3, sc) in next st *(button lp)*, working across next side in ends of sc rows, *ch 4, sl st in next sc row, rep from * 3 [5] times, ch 4, sk heel seam, sl st in end of next sc row. Fasten off.

Finishing

Referring to photo for placement, sew 1 button to center of each Slipper. ●

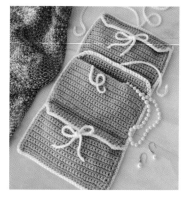

Jewelry Roll
Continued from page 59

Note: Sides of Pockets and lower edge of 3rd Pocket will be sewn later.

Outer Trim

Rnd 1 (RS): Hold Outer Section with RS facing and starting ch at top, working through both thicknesses at same time and removing pins as work progresses, join sage with sc in first unused lp of starting ch, ch 1, 2 sc in same lp, working across in rem unused lps of starting ch, sc in each lp across to last lp, 3 sc in last lp, working across next side in ends of rows, sc evenly sp across to next corner, working across row 64, 3 sc in first sc, sc in each sc across to last sc, 3 sc in last sc, working across next side in ends of rows, sc evenly sp across to joining sc, join in joining sc. Fasten off.

Rnd 2: Join off-white with sc in 2nd sc of any corner, sc in same sc, sc in each sc across to 2nd sc of next corner, [2 sc in 2nd sc of corner, sc in each sc across to 2nd sc of next corner] twice, 2 sc in 2nd sc of corner, sc in each sc across to beg sc, join in beg sc. Fasten off.

Fasten off surface sl sts as follows: Insert hook from WS to RS of work, draw dropped lp of last surface sl st of 1 Horizontal Trim through to WS. Rep with last surface sl st of 2nd Horizontal Trim.

Weave ends under sts of Outer Trim.

Flap

Make 3.

Row 1 (RS): Beg at top with sage and leaving 12-inch end for sewing, ch 29, sc in 2nd ch from hook, sc in each ch across, turn. *(28 sc)*

Row 2: Ch 1, **sc dec** *(see Stitch Guide)* in first 2 sc, sc in each sc across to last 2 sc, sc dec in last 2 sc, turn. *(26 sc)*

Row 3: Ch 1, sc dec in first 2 sc, sc in each sc across to last 2 sc, sc dec in last 2 sc, turn. *(24 sc)*

Row 4: Ch 1, sc dec in first 2 sc, sc in each sc across to last 2 sc, sc dec in last 2 sc. Fasten off. *(22 sc)*

Edging

Hold Flap with RS facing, **join** *(see Pattern Notes)* off-white in edge of row 1, working across side in ends of rem rows, sc in each row, working across row 4, 2 sc in first sc, sc in each sc across to last sc, 2 sc in last sc, working across next side in ends of rows, sc in each row. Fasten off.

Assembly

With tapestry needle and 12-inch end, sew 1 Flap to unused lps of row 18. Rep with rem Flaps on rows 40 and 62.

Flap Tie

Make 3.

Join off-white in center of 1 Flap, ch 35, fasten off. Tie knot in end, pull tight and trim.

Rep on rem 2 Flaps.

Pocket Tie

Make 3.

Join off-white in center of 1 Pocket, directly below Flap Tie, ch 35, fasten off. Tie knot in end, pull tight and trim.

Rep for rem 2 Pockets.

Jewelry Roll Tie

With off-white, ch 85, hold Outer Section with WS facing, sl st in center of Outer Trim on top edge, ch 60, fasten off. Tie knots in ends, pull tight and trim.

Finishing

Starting at lower edge, fold Jewelry Roll in thirds, wrapping longer end of Jewelry Roll Tie around Jewelry Roll. Pull ends up even and tie in bow. ●

Just for Babies

These simple designs will make your little one look like a million dollars!

Serenity Blue Dress

Design by *Shirley Patterson*

Skill Level

■■□□
EASY

Finished Size
Instructions given fit
infant's size 6–9 months

Finished Garment Measurement
Chest: 16 inches

Materials
• Bernat Softee Baby light
(light worsted) weight
yarn (5 oz/468 yds/140g
 per ball):
    3 balls #02002 pale blue
• Size D/3/3.25mm
crochet hook or size
needed to obtain gauge
• Tapestry needle
• Sewing needle
• 2 yds ⅛-inch blue
satin ribbon
• 3 blue ½-inch
flat buttons
• 1 blue satin ribbon
rose trim
• Matching sewing thread

Gauge
5 sts = 1 inch

Pattern Notes
Weave in ends as work progresses.

Join with slip stitch as indicated unless otherwise stated.

Chain-3 at beginning of rows counts as first double crochet unless otherwise stated.

Special Stitches
Beginning shell: Ch 3, (dc, ch 2, 2 dc) in indicated place.

Shell: (2 dc, ch 2, 2 dc) in indicated place.

Cluster (cl): Holding back last lp on hook, 3 tr in indicated sp, yo and draw through all 4 lps on hook.

Large cluster (lg cl): Holding back last lp on hook, 3 tr in each of 2 indicated sps, yo and draw through all 7 lps on hook.

Picot: Ch 3, sl st in last st.

Dress

Yoke

Row 1 (RS): Ch 98, dc in 5th ch from hook *(beg 4 sk chs count as a dc)*, dc in each of next 9 chs, ch 2, [dc in each of next 10 chs, ch 1, sk next ch, dc in each of next 10 chs, ch 2] 3 times, dc in each of last 11 chs, turn. *(82 dc)*

Row 2: Ch 3 (*see Pattern Notes*), dc in each of next 10 dc, **shell** (*see Special Stitches*) in next ch sp, [dc in each of next 9 dc, ch 1, sk next dc, dc in next ch sp, ch 1, sk next dc, dc in each of next 9 dc, shell in next ch sp] 3 times, dc in each of last 10 dc, dc in 4th ch of beg 4 sk chs, turn.

Row 3: Ch 3, dc in each of next 12 dc, shell in ch-2 sp of next shell, *dc in each of next 10 dc, ch 1, sk next dc, dc in next ch-1 sp, dc in next dc, dc in next ch-1 sp, ch 1, sk next dc, dc in each of next 10 dc, shell in ch-2 sp of next shell, rep from * twice, dc in each of last 12 dc, dc in 3rd ch of beg ch-3, turn.

Row 4: Ch 3, dc in each of next 14 dc, shell in ch-2 sp of next shell, *dc in each of next 11 dc, ch 1, sk next dc, dc in next ch-1 sp, dc in each of next 3 dc, dc in next ch-1 sp, ch 1, sk next dc, dc in each of next 11 dc, shell in ch-2 sp of next shell, rep from * twice, dc in each of last 14 dc, dc in 3rd ch of beg ch-3, turn.

Row 5: Ch 3, dc in each of next 16 dc, shell in ch-2 sp of next shell, *dc in each of next 12 dc, ch 1, sk next dc, dc in next ch-1 sp, dc in each of next 2 dc, ch 1, sk next dc, dc in each of next 2 dc, dc in next ch-1 sp, ch 1, sk next dc, dc in each of next 12 dc, shell in ch-2 sp of next shell, rep from * twice, dc in each of last 16 dc, dc in 3rd ch of beg ch-3, turn.

Row 6: Ch 3, dc in each of next 18 dc, shell in ch-2 sp of next shell, *dc in each of next 14 dc, ch 1, sk next dc, dc in each of next 2 dc, dc in next ch-1 sp, dc in each of next 2 dc, ch 1, sk next dc, dc in next ch-1 sp, dc in each of next 14 dc, shell in ch-2 sp of next shell, rep from * twice, dc in each of last 18 dc, dc in 3rd ch of beg ch-3, turn.

Row 7: Ch 3, dc in each of next 20 dc, shell in ch-2 sp of next shell, *dc in each of next 17 dc, dc in next ch-1 sp, ch 1, sk next dc, dc in each of next 3 dc, ch 1, sk next dc, dc in next ch-1 sp, dc in each of next 17 dc, shell in ch-2 sp of next shell, rep from * twice, dc in each of last 21 dc, dc in 3rd ch of beg ch-3, turn.

Row 8: Ch 3, dc in each of next 22 dc, shell in ch-2 sp of next shell, *dc in each of next 20 dc, dc in next ch-1 sp, ch 1, sk next dc, dc in dc, ch 1, sk next dc, dc in next ch-1 sp, dc in each of next 20 dc, shell in ch-2 sp of next shell, rep from * twice, dc in each of last 23 dc, dc in 3rd ch of beg ch-3, turn.

Armhole

Row 9: Ch 3, dc in each dc to ch-2 sp of next shell, 2 dc in ch-2 sp of next shell, ch 7, sk next 2 ch-1 sps, 2 dc in ch-2 sp of next shell, dc in each of next 23 dc, dc in next ch-1 sp, ch 1, sk next dc, dc in next ch-1 sp, dc in each of next 23 dc, 2 dc in ch-2 sp of next shell, ch 7, sk next 1 ch-1 sp, 2 dc in ch-2 sp of next shell, dc in each rem dc across, turn.

Row 10: Ch 2, hdc in first dc, ch 1, sk next dc, *hdc in next dc, ch 1, sk next dc, rep from * across to beg ch-3, hdc in 3rd ch of beg ch-3, turn. (60 *ch-1 sps*)

Row 11: Ch 1, working in hdc and in chs, work 119 sc evenly sp across, turn. (119 *sc*)

Skirt

Row 12: Ch 3, shell in first sc, sk next 4 sc, [dc in next sc, sk next 2 sc, shell in next sc, sk next 2 sc] 6 times, dc in next sc, sk next 3 sc, shell in next sc, sk next 2 sc, dc in next sc, sk next 3 sc, shell in next sc, sk next 2 sc, dc in next sc, sk next 2 sc, shell in next sc, sk next 2 sc, dc in next sc, sk next 3 sc, shell in next sc, sk next 2 sc, dc in next sc, sk next 3 sc, shell in next sc, sk next 2 sc, dc in next sc, sk next 2 sc, shell in next sc, sk next 2 sc, dc in next sc, sk next 3 sc, shell in next sc, sk next 2 sc, dc in next sc, sk next 2 sc, shell in next sc, sk next 2 sc, dc in next sc, sk next 3 sc, shell in next sc, sk next 2 sc, dc in next sc, sk

next 2 sc, shell in next sc, sc, sk next 4 sc, dc in next sc, turn.

Rnd 13: Now working in rnds, sl st in each of first 3 dc, sl st in next ch-2 sp, **beg shell** *(see Special Stitches)* in same sp, ch 2, 7 dc in next ch-2 sp, ch 2, [shell in ch-2 sp of next shell, ch 2, 7 dc in next ch-2 sp, ch 2] 7 times, shell in ch-2 sp of next shell, ch 2, 7 dc in ch-2 sp of next shell, ch 7, **join** *(see Pattern Notes)* in 3rd ch of beg ch-3.

Rnd 14: Sl st in next dc, sl st in next ch-2 sp, beg shell in same sp, ch 1, [dc in next dc, ch 1] 7 times, *shell in ch-2 sp of next shell, ch 1, [dc in next dc, ch 1] 7 times, rep from * 7 times, join in 3rd ch of beg ch-3.

Rnd 15: Sl st in next dc, sl st in next ch-2 sp, beg shell in same sp, ch 3, [sc in next ch-1 sp, ch 3] 6 times, *shell in ch-2 sp of next shell, ch 3, [sc in next ch-1 sp, ch 3] 6 times, rep from * 7 times, join in 3rd ch of beg ch-3.

Rnd 16: Sl st in next dc, sl st in next ch-2 sp, beg shell in same sp, ch 3, [sc in next ch-3 sp, ch 3] 5 times, *shell in ch-2 sp of next shell, ch 3, [sc in next ch-3 sp, ch 3] 5 times, rep from * 7 times, join in 3rd ch of beg ch-3.

Rnd 17: Sl st in next dc, sl st in next ch-2 sp, beg shell in same sp, ch 3, [sc in next ch-3 sp, ch 3] 4 times, *shell in ch-2 sp of next shell, ch 3, [sc in next ch-3 sp, ch 3] 4 times, rep from * 7 times, join in 3rd ch of beg ch-3.

Rnd 18: Sl st in next dc, sl st in next ch-2 sp, (beg shell, ch 2, 2 dc) in same sp, ch 3, [sc in next ch-3 sp, ch 3] 3 times, *(shell, ch 2, 2 dc) in ch-2 sp of next shell, ch 3, [sc in next ch-3 sp, ch 3] 3 times, rep from * 7 times, join in 3rd ch of beg ch-3.

Rnd 19: Sl st in next dc, sl st in next ch-2 sp, beg shell in same sp, ch 3, shell in next ch-2 sp, ch 3, [sc in next ch-3 sp, ch 3] twice, *[shell in next ch-2 sp, ch 3] twice, [sc in next ch-3 sp, ch 3] twice, rep from * 7 times, join in 3rd ch of beg ch-3.

Rnd 20: Sl st in next dc, sl st in next ch-2 sp, beg shell in same sp, ch 1, (dc, ch 3, dc) in 2nd ch of next ch-3 sp, ch 1, shell in ch-2 sp of next shell, ch 3, sc in next ch-3 sp, ch 3, *shell in ch-2 sp of next shell, ch 1, (dc, ch 3, dc) in 2nd ch of next ch-3 sp, ch 1, shell in ch-2 sp of next shell, ch 3, sc in next ch-3 sp, ch 3, rep from * 7 times, join in 3rd ch of beg ch-3.

Rnd 21: Sl st in next dc, sl st in next ch-2 sp, beg shell in same sp, ch 1, dc in next dc, 7 dc in next ch-3 sp, dc in next dc, ch 1, shell in ch-2 sp of next shell, *shell in ch-2 sp of next shell, ch 1, dc in next dc, 7 dc in next ch-3 sp, dc in next dc, ch 1, shell in ch-2 sp of next shell, rep from * 7 times, join in 3rd ch of beg ch-3.

Rnd 22: Sl st in next dc, sl st in next ch-2 sp, beg shell in same sp, ch 1, [dc in next dc, ch 1] 9 times, shell in ch-2 sp of next shell, *shell in ch-2 sp of next shell, ch 1, [dc in next dc, ch 1] 9 times, shell in ch-2 sp of next shell, rep from * 7 times, join in 3rd ch of beg ch-3.

Rnd 23: Sl st in next dc, sl st in next ch-2 sp, beg shell in same sp, ch 3, [sc in next ch-1 sp, ch 3] 8 times, shell in ch-2 sp of next shell, *shell in ch-2 sp of next shell, ch 3, [sc in next ch-1 sp, ch 3] 8 times, shell in ch-2 sp of next shell, rep from * 7 times, join in 3rd ch of beg ch-3.

Rnd 24: Sl st in next dc, sl st in next ch-2 sp, beg shell in same sp, ch 3, [sc in next ch-3 sp, ch 3] 7 times, shell in ch-2 sp of next shell, *shell in ch-2 sp of next shell, ch 3, [sc in next ch-3 sp, ch 3] 7 times, shell in ch-2 sp of next shell, rep from * 7 times, join in 3rd ch of beg ch-3.

Rnd 25: Sl st in next dc, sl st in next ch-2 sp, beg shell in same sp, ch 3, [sc in next ch-3 sp, ch 3] 6 times, shell in ch-2 sp of next shell, ch 1, (dc, ch 3, dc) in 2nd ch of next ch-3 sp, ch 1, *shell in ch-2 sp of next shell, ch 3, [sc in next ch-3 sp, ch 3] 6 times, shell in ch-2 sp of next shell, ch 1, (dc, ch 3, dc) in 2nd ch of next ch-3 sp, ch 1, rep from * 7 times, join in 3rd ch of beg ch-3.

Rnd 26: Sl st in next dc, sl st in next ch-2 sp, beg shell in same sp, ch 3, [sc in next ch-3 sp, ch 3] 5 times, shell in ch-2 sp of next shell, ch 3, dc in next dc, 5 dc in next ch sp, dc in next dc, ch 3, *shell in ch-2 sp of next shell, ch 3, [sc in next ch-3 sp, ch 3] 5 times, shell in ch-2 sp of next shell, ch 3, dc in next dc, 5 dc in next ch sp, dc in next dc, ch 3, rep from * 7 times, join in 3rd ch of beg ch-3.

Continued on page 92

Boy Blue Sunday Suit

Designs by *Shirley Patterson*

Skill Level

INTERMEDIATE

Finished Size
Instructions given fit infant's size 6–9 months

Finished Garment Measurement
Chest: 22 inches

Materials
• Bernat Softee Baby light (light worsted) weight yarn (5 oz/468 yds/140g per ball):
  3 balls #02002 pale blue
• Size D/3/3.25mm crochet hook or size needed to obtain gauge
• Tapestry needle
• Sewing needle
• 8 flat ¾-inch blue buttons
• 13-inch piece of ¼-inch elastic
• Stitch markers
• Matching sewing thread

Gauge

6 dc = 1 inch

Pattern Notes

Weave in ends as work progresses.

Join with slip stitch as indicated unless otherwise stated.

Pants

Left Leg

Rnd 1 (RS): Ch 71, **join** (*see Pattern Notes*) in first ch to form a ring, ch 3, dc in same ch as joining, dc in each rem ch around, sk beg ch-3, join in first dc. (*71 dc*)

Rnd 2: Ch 3, dc in same dc as joining, dc in each of next 16 dc, ch 1, sk next dc, dc in each of next 53 dc, sk beg ch-3, join in first dc. (*70 dc, 1 ch-1 sp*)

Rnd 3: Ch 3, dc in same dc as joining, dc in each of next 15 dc, ch 1, sk next dc, dc in next ch-1 sp, ch 1, sk next dc, dc in each of next 52 dc, sk beg ch-3, join in first dc.

Rnd 4: Ch 3, dc in same dc as joining, dc in each of next 14 dc, ch 1, sk next dc, dc in next ch-1 sp, dc in next dc, dc in next ch-1 sp, ch 1, sk next dc, dc in each of next 51 dc, sk beg ch-3, join in first dc.

Rnd 5: Ch 3, dc in same dc as joining, dc in each of next 13 dc, ch 1, sk next dc, dc in next ch-1 sp, dc in each of next 3 dc,

dc in next ch-1 sp, ch 1, sk next dc, dc in each of next 50 dc, sk beg ch-3, join in first dc.

Rnd 6: Ch 3, dc in same dc as joining, dc in each of next 12 dc, ch 1, sk next dc, dc in next ch-1 sp, dc in each of next 2 dc, ch 1, sk next dc, dc in each of next 2 dc, dc in next ch-1 sp, ch 1, sk next dc, dc in each of next 49 dc, sk beg ch-3, join in first dc.

Rnd 7: Ch 3, dc in same dc as joining, dc in each of next 12 dc, dc in next ch-1 sp, ch 1, sk next dc, dc in each of next 2 dc, dc in next ch-1 sp, dc in each of next 2 dc, ch 1, sk next dc, dc in next ch-1 sp, dc in each of next 49 dc, sk beg ch-3, join in first dc.

Rnd 8: Ch 3, dc in same dc as joining, dc in each of next 13 dc, dc in next ch-1 sp, ch 1, sk next dc, dc in each of next 3 dc, ch 1, sk next dc, dc in next ch-1 sp, dc in each of next 50 dc, sk beg ch-3, join in first dc.

Rnd 9: Ch 3, dc in same dc as joining, dc in each of next 14 dc, dc in next ch-1 sp, ch 1, sk next dc, dc in next dc, ch 1, sk next dc, dc in next ch-1 sp, dc in each of next 51 dc, sk beg ch-3, join in first dc.

Rnd 10: Ch 3, dc in same dc as joining, dc in each of next 15 dc, dc in next ch-1 sp, ch 1, sk next dc, dc in next ch-1 sp, dc in each of next 52 dc, sk beg ch-3, join in first dc. *(70 dc, 1 ch-1 sp)*

Rnd 11: Ch 3, dc in same dc as joining, dc in each rem dc and in each ch-1 sp around, sk beg ch-3, join in first dc. *(71 dc)*

Rnd 12: Rep rnd 11. Fasten off.

Right Leg

Rnd 1 (RS): Ch 71, join in first ch to form a ring, ch 3, dc in same ch as joining, dc in each rem ch around, sk beg ch-3, join in first dc. *(71 dc)*

Rnd 2: Ch 3, dc in same dc as joining, dc in each of next 52 dc, ch 1, sk next dc, dc in each of next 17 dc, sk beg ch-3, join in first dc. *(70 dc, 1 ch-1 sp)*

Rnd 3: Ch 3, dc in same dc as joining, dc in each of next 51 dc, ch 1, sk next dc, dc in next ch-1 sp, ch 1, sk next dc, dc in each of next 16 dc, sk beg ch-3, join in first dc.

Rnd 4: Ch 3, dc in same dc as joining, dc in each of next 50 dc, ch 1, sk next dc, dc in next ch-1 sp, dc in next dc, dc in next ch-1 sp, ch 1, sk next dc, dc in each of next 51 dc, sk beg ch-3, join in first dc.

Rnd 5: Ch 3, dc in same dc as joining, dc in each of next 49 dc, ch 1, sk next dc, dc in next ch-1 sp, dc in each of next 3 dc, dc in next ch-1 sp, ch 1, sk next dc, dc in each of next 14 dc, sk beg ch-3, join in first dc.

Rnd 6: Ch 3, dc in same dc as joining, dc in each of next 48 dc, ch 1, sk next dc, dc in next ch-1 sp, dc in each of next 2 dc, ch 1, sk next dc, dc in each of next 2 dc, dc in next ch-1 sp, ch 1, sk next dc, dc in each of next 13 dc, sk beg ch-3, join in first dc.

Rnd 7: Ch 3, dc in same dc as joining, dc in each of next 48 dc, dc in next ch-1 sp, ch 1, sk next dc, dc in each of next 2 dc, dc in next ch-1 sp, dc in each of next 2 dc, ch 1, sk next dc, dc in next ch-1 sp, dc in each of next 13 dc, sk beg ch-3, join in first dc.

Rnd 8: Ch 3, dc in same dc as joining, dc in each of next 40 dc, dc in next ch-1 sp, ch 1, sk next dc, dc in each of next 3 dc, ch 1, sk next dc, dc in next ch-1 sp, dc in each of next 14 dc, sk beg ch-3, join in first dc.

Rnd 9: Ch 3, dc in same dc as joining, dc in each of next 50 dc, dc in next ch-1 sp, ch 1, sk next dc, dc in next dc, ch 1, sk next dc, dc in next ch-1 sp, dc in each of next 15 dc, sk beg ch-3, join in first dc.

Rnd 10: Ch 3, dc in same dc as joining, dc in each of next 51 dc, dc in next ch-1 sp, ch 1, sk next dc, dc in next ch-1 sp, dc in each of next 16 dc, sk beg ch-3, join in first dc.

Note: Mark 37th dc.

Rnd 11: Ch 3, dc in same dc as joining, dc in each rem dc and in each ch-1 sp around, sk beg ch-3, join in first dc. *(71 dc)*

Rnd 12: Rep rnd 11. Fasten off.

Crotch

Row 1 (RS): Ch 2, sc in 2nd ch from hook, turn. *(1 sc)*

Row 2: Ch 1, 2 sc in sc, turn. *(2 sc)*

Row 3: Ch 1, 2 sc in first sc, sc in last sc, turn. *(3 sc)*

Row 4: Ch 1, 2 sc in first sc, sc in each rem sc across, turn. *(4 sc)*

Rows 5–7: Rep row 4. *(7 sc at end of last row)*

Row 8: Ch 1, **sc dec** *(see Stitch Guide)* in first 2 sc, sc in each rem sc across, turn. *(6 sc)*

Rows 9–13: Rep row 8. At end of last row, fasten off. *(1 sc at end of last row)*

Assembly

Hold Crotch and Right Leg with RS tog and row 7 of Crotch matching first dc of rnd 12 of Right Leg, working in ends of rows of Crotch and in corresponding dc of rnd 12 at same time, **join** *(see Pattern Notes)* yarn in end of rnd 12 of Right Leg, sl st in each row across. Fasten off. Join Left Leg to opposite side of Crotch in same manner.

Body

Note: *Sew ends of elastic together and set aside.*

Rnd 1 (RS): Hold piece with RS facing, join yarn in marked dc of Left Leg, ch 3, dc in same dc as joining, dc in each of next 27 dc, **dc dec** *(see Stitch Guide)* in next dc, in tip of Crotch and in next dc, dc in each of next 58 dc, dc dec in next dc, in tip of Crotch and in next dc, dc in each rem st around to beg ch-3, sk beg ch-3, join in first dc. *(118 dc)*

Rnd 2: Ch 3, dc in same dc as joining, dc in each rem dc around, sk beg ch-3, join in first dc.

Rnds 3–9: Rep rnd 2.

Rnd 10: Ch 3, dc in same dc as joining, dc in each of next 16 dc, ch 1, sk next dc, dc in each of next 22 dc, ch 1, sk next dc, dc in each of last 77 dc, sk beg ch-3, join in first dc.

Rnd 11: Ch 3, dc in same dc as joining, dc in each of next 15 dc, ch 1, sk next dc, dc in next ch-1 sp, ch 1, sk next dc, dc in each of next 20 dc, ch 1, sk next dc, dc in next ch-1 sp, ch 1, sk next dc, dc in each of last 76 dc, sk beg ch-3, join in first dc.

Rnd 12: Ch 3, dc in same dc as joining, dc in each of next 14 dc, ch 1, sk next dc, dc in next ch-1 sp, dc in next dc, dc in next ch-1 sp, ch 1, sk next dc, dc in each of next 18 dc, ch 1, sk next dc, dc in next ch-1 sp, dc in next dc, dc in next ch-1 sp, ch 1, sk next dc, dc in each of last 75 dc, sk beg ch-3, join in first dc.

Rnd 13: Ch 3, dc in same dc as joining, dc in each of next 13 dc, ch 1, sk next dc, dc in next ch-1 sp, dc in each of next 3 dc, dc in next ch-1 sp, ch 1, sk next dc, dc in each of next 16 dc, ch 1, sk next dc, dc in next ch-1 sp, dc in each of next 3 dc, dc in next ch-1 sp, ch 1, sk next dc, dc in each of last 74 dc, sk beg ch-3, join in first dc.

Continued on page 95

Baby Boy Sheriff

Design by *Jewdy Lambert*

Skill Level
◼◼◼▭
INTERMEDIATE

Finished Sizes
Instructions fit size infant's size 3 months; changes for infant's sizes 6 and 12 months are in [ ].

Finished Garment Measurements
Chest: 26 [28, 30] inches

Materials
• Plymouth Yarn Encore Colorspun medium (worsted) weight yarn (3½ oz/200 yds/100g per ball):
  2 [3, 3] balls #7172 orange/brown/grey variegated (MC)
• Medium (worsted) weight yarn:
  4 yds each brown variegated (CC) and tan (A)
• Size G/6/4mm crochet hook or size needed to obtain gauge
• Tapestry needle

Gauge
4 sts = 1 inch

Pattern Notes
Weave in ends as work progresses.

Join with slip stitch as indicated unless otherwise stated.

Chain-2 at beginning of rows counts as first half double crochet unless otherwise stated.

Chain-3 at beginning of rows counts as first double crochet unless otherwise stated.

Special Stitch
Popcorn (pc): Yo, [draw up lp in indicated st] 3 times, yo and draw through all lps on hook.

Jacket
Ribbing
Row 1 (RS): Starting at lower edge with MC, ch 98 [102, 106], dc in 4th ch from hook *(beg 3 sk chs counts as a dc)*, dc in each rem ch across, turn. *(96 [100, 104] dc)*

Row 2: Ch 2 *(see Pattern Notes)*, *bpdc *(see Stitch Guide)* around next dc, sc in next dc, rep from * across, turn.

Row 3: Ch 2, *fpdc *(see Stitch Guide)* around next st, sc in next st, rep from * across, turn.

Size 3 Months Only

Row 4: Rep row 2.

Sizes 6 Months & 12 Months Only

Rows [4 & 5]: Rep rows 2 and 3.

Body

Row 1: Ch 3 (*see Pattern Notes*), dc in each st across, turn.

Rows 2–7 [2–9, 2–11]: Rep row 1.

Right Front

Row 1 (RS): Ch 3, dc in each of next 23 [24, 25] dc, leaving rem dc unworked, turn. (*24 [25, 26] dc*)

Row 2: Ch 3, dc in each dc across, turn.

Rows 3–8 [3–10, 3–12]: Rep row 2.

Neck Shaping

Row 1 (RS): Ch 1, sk first sc, sl st in each of next 2 sc, sc in each of next 2 [3, 3] dc, dc in each of next 19 [19, 20] dc, turn. (*24 [25, 26] sts*)

Row 2: Ch 3, dc in each of first 15 [15, 16] sts, sc in each of next 3 sts, leaving rem sts unworked, turn.

Row 3: Ch 1, sc in each of first 3 sc, dc in each of next 14 [15, 16] sts, turn.

Size 3 Months Only

Row 4: Rep row 2. Fasten off.

Size 6 Months Only

Rows [4 & 5]: Rep rows 2 and 3. At end of last row, fasten off.

Size 12 Months Only

Rows [4 & 5]: Rep rows 2 and 3.

Row [6]: Rep row 2. Fasten off.

Back

Row 1 (RS): Join MC in next unused dc on last row of Body from Right Front, ch 3, dc in each of next 47 [49, 51] dc, leaving rem dc unworked, turn. (*48 [50, 52] dc*)

Row 2: Ch 3, dc in each dc across, turn.

Rows 3–10 [3–11, 3–12]: Rep row 2. At end of last row, fasten off.

Left Front

Row 1 (RS): Join MC in next unused dc on last row of Body from Back, ch 3, dc in each rem dc across, turn. (*24 [25, 26] dc*)

Continued on page 103

Sunday Pink

Designs by *Lucille LaFlamme*

Skill Level
■■□□ EASY

Finished Sizes
Hat: 16 inches in circumference, excluding Brim

Dress: Instructions given fit infant's size 12 months (9 inches long from waist)

Purse: 6 inches x 6½ inches, excluding handle

Materials
Hat
• Red Heart Soft Baby Steps medium (worsted) weight yarn (5 oz/256 yds/142g per skein):
  1 skein #9700 baby pink
• Size F/5/3.75mm crochet hook or size needed to obtain gauge
• Tapestry needle
• Sewing needle
• 1 yd ¼-inch wide white ribbon
• 1 white satin ribbon rose
• Matching sewing thread

Dress
• Red Heart Soft Baby Steps medium (worsted) weight yarn (5 oz/256 yds/142g per skein):
  1 skein #9700 baby pink
• Size F/5/3.75mm crochet hook or size needed to obtain gauge
• Tapestry needle
• Sewing needle
• Purchased 12-month-old size white shirt
• Matching sewing thread

Hat
Gauge
6 dc = 1 inch

Pattern Notes
Weave in ends as work progresses.

Join with slip stitch as indicated unless otherwise stated.

Chain-3 at beginning of rounds counts as first double crochet unless otherwise stated.

Special Stitch
Picot: Ch 3, sl st in last st made.

Hat
Rnd 1 (RS): Ch 3, **join** (*see Pattern Notes*) in first ch to form a ring, **ch 3** (*see Pattern Notes*), 16 dc in ring, join in 3rd ch of beg ch-3. (*17 dc*)

Rnd 2: Ch 3, dc in same ch as joining, 2 dc in each dc around, join in 3rd ch of beg ch-3. (*34 dc*)

Rnd 3: Ch 3, dc in same ch as joining, 2 dc in next dc, *dc in next dc, 2 dc in each of next 2 dc, rep from * around to last 2 dc, dc in each of last 2 dc, join in 3rd ch of beg ch-3. (*56 dc*)

Rnd 4: Ch 3, dc in each of next 3 dc, *2 dc in next dc, dc in each of next 4 dc, rep from * around to last 2 dc, 2 dc in next dc, dc in last dc, join in 3rd ch of beg ch-3. *(67 dc)*

Rnd 5: Ch 3, dc in each of next 7 dc, *2 dc in next dc, dc in each of next 4 dc, rep from * around to last 2 dc, 2 dc in next dc, dc in last dc, join in 3rd ch of beg ch-3. *(78 dc)*

Rnd 6: Ch 3, dc in each dc around, join in 3rd ch of beg ch-3.

Rnd 7: Ch 3, dc in each of next 4 dc, dc dec in next 2 dc, *dc in each of next 5 dc, dc dec in next 2 dc, rep from * around to last dc, dc in last dc, join in 3rd ch of beg ch-3.

Rnds 8 & 9: Rep rnd 6.

Brim

Rnd 10: Ch 3, dc in each of next 3 dc, *2 dc in next dc, dc in each of next 3 dc, rep from * around, join in 3rd ch of beg ch-3. *(84 dc)*

Rnd 11: Ch 3, dc in each of next 3 dc, *2 dc in next dc, dc in each of next 3 dc, rep from * around, join in 3rd ch of beg ch-3. *(104 dc)*

Rnd 12: Ch 3, [2 dc in next dc, dc in each of next 3 dc] 25 times, 2 dc in next dc, dc in each of next 2 dc, join in 3rd ch of beg ch-3. *(130 dc)*

Rnd 13: Ch 1, sc in same ch as joining, **picot** *(see Special Stitch)*, ch 3, sk next 2 dc, *sc in next dc, picot, ch 3, sk next 2 dc, rep from * around, join in first sc. Fasten off.

Flower

Ch 4, join in first ch to form a ring, [ch 3, dc in ring, ch 3, sl st in ring] 5 times. Fasten off.

Finishing

Sew white silk ribbon rose to center of Flower. Sew Flower to top of Hat.

Cut 27-inch length of ribbon. Weave through rnd 8 and tie in bow.

Dress

Gauge

6 sc = 1 inch

Pattern Notes

Weave in ends as work progresses.

Join with slip stitch as indicated unless otherwise stated.

Chain-3 at beginning of rounds counts as first double crochet unless otherwise stated.

Chain-5 at beginning of rounds counts as first double crochet and chain-2 space unless otherwise stated.

Special Stitches

Beginning cluster (beg cl): Ch 3, keeping back last lp of each dc, 2 dc in indicated sp, yo and draw through all 3 lps on hook.

Cluster (cl): Keeping back last lp of each dc, 3 dc in indicated st, yo and draw through all 4 lps on hook.

Picot: Ch 3, sl st in last st made.

Dress

Skirt

Rnd 1 (RS): Ch 100, **join** (*see Pattern Notes*) in first ch, being careful not to twist ch, sc in same ch as joining, sc in each rem ch around, join in beg sc. (*100 sc*)

Rnd 2: Ch 1, 3 sc in first sc, *sc in each of next 3 sc, 2 sc in next sc, rep from * around to last 3 sc, sc in each of last 3 sc, join in beg sc. (*126 sc*)

Rnd 3: Ch 3, sk next 5 sc, *(dc, ch 1, dc, ch 3, dc, ch 1, dc) in next sc, sk next 5 sc, rep from * 19 times, (dc, ch 1, dc, ch 3, dc, ch 1) in same sc as beg ch-3, join in 3rd ch of beg ch-3.

Rnd 4: Sl st in next dc, sl st in next ch-1 sp, sl st in next ch-3 sp, **beg cl** (*see Special Stitches*) in same sp, ch 3, **cl** (*see Special Stitches*) in same sp, ch 3, *(cl, ch 3, cl) in next ch-3 sp, ch 3, rep from * around, join in top of beg cl.

Rnd 5: Sl st in next ch-3 sp, beg cl in same sp, ch 2, dc in next ch-3 sp, ch 2, *cl in next ch-3 sp, ch 2, dc in next ch-3 sp, ch 2, rep from * around, join in top of beg cl.

Rnd 6: Ch 5 (*see Pattern Notes*), (dc, ch 1, dc) in next dc, ch 2, *dc in next cl, ch 2, (dc, ch 1, dc) in next dc, ch 2, rep from * around, join in 3rd ch of beg ch-5.

Rnd 7: Sl st in each of next 4 chs, sl st in next dc, sl st in next ch-1 sp, ch 4, (dc, ch 3, dc, ch 1, dc) in same sp, ch 1, sk next 2 ch-2 sps, *(dc, ch 1, dc, ch 3, dc, ch 1, dc) in next ch-1 sp, ch 1, sk next 2 ch-2 sps, rep from * around, join in 3rd ch of beg ch-4.

Rnd 8: Sl st in next ch, sl st in next dc, sl st in next ch-3 sp, (beg cl, ch 3, cl) in same sp, ch 3, *(cl, ch 3, cl) in next ch-3 sp, ch 3, rep from * around, join in top of beg cl.

Rnd 9: Sl st in next ch-3 sp, beg cl in same sp, ch 3, dc in next ch-3 sp, ch 3, *cl in next ch-3 sp, ch 3, dc in next ch-3 sp, ch 3, rep from * around, join in top of beg cl.

Rnd 10: Ch 5, (dc, ch 2, dc) in next dc, ch 2, *dc in next cl, ch 2, (dc, ch 2, dc) in next dc, ch 2, rep from * around, join in 3rd ch of beg ch-5.

Rnd 11: Sl st in each of next 2 chs, sl st in next dc, sl st in next ch-2 sp, ch 4, (dc, ch 3, dc, ch 1, dc) in same sp, ch 1, sk next 2 ch-2 sps, *(dc, ch 1, dc, ch 3, dc, ch 1, dc) in next ch-2 sp, ch 1, sk next 2 ch-2 sps, rep from * around, join in 3rd ch of beg ch-4.

Rnds 12–15: Rep rnds 8–11.

Rnds 16 & 17: Rep rnds 8 and 9.

Edging

Rnd 1 (RS): Ch 1, sc in same beg cl, ch 3, dc in next dc, ch 3, *sc in next cl, ch 3, dc in next dc, ch 3, rep from * around, join in beg sc.

Rnd 2: Ch 1, sc in same sc as joining, ch 1, (hdc, ch 1, dc) in next ch-3 sp, ch 1, (dc, **picot**—*see Special Stitches*, dc) in next dc, ch 1, (dc, ch 1, hdc) in next ch-3 sp, ch 1, *sc in next sc, ch 1, (hdc, ch 1, dc) in next ch-3 sp, ch 1, (dc, picot, dc) in next dc, ch 1, (dc, ch 1, hdc) in next ch-3 sp, ch 1, rep from * around, join in beg sc. Fasten off.

Collar Trim

Crochet a ch to measure around collar of shirt plus ½ inch, having a multiple of 6, (dc, ch 1, dc, picot, dc, ch 1, dc) in 4th ch from hook, ch 1, sk next 2 chs, sc in next ch, ch 1, sk next 2 chs, *(dc, ch 1, dc, picot, dc, ch 1, dc) in next ch, ch 1, sk next 2 chs, sc in next ch, ch 1, sk next 2 chs, rep from * across to last 2 chs, (dc, ch 1, dc, picot, dc, ch 1, dc) in next ch, ch 1, sc in last ch. Fasten off.

Sleeve Trim

Make 2.

Crochet a ch to measure around sleeve of shirt plus ½ inch, having a multiple of 6, (dc, ch 1, dc, picot, dc, ch 1, dc) in 4th ch from hook, ch 1, sk next 2 chs, sc in next ch, ch 1, sk next 2 chs, *(dc, ch 1, dc, picot, dc, ch 1, dc) in next ch, ch 1, sk next 2 chs, sc in next ch, ch 1, sk next 2 chs, rep from * across to last 2 chs, (dc, ch 1, dc, picot, dc, ch 1, dc) in next ch, ch 1, sc in last ch. Fasten off.

Finishing

Sew Skirt, Collar Trim and Sleeve Trims to shirt.

Purse

Gauge

Rnd 1 = 1 inches

Pattern Notes

Weave in ends as work progresses.

Join with slip stitch as indicated unless otherwise stated.

Continued on page 105

Materials

Purse
- Red Heart Soft Baby Steps medium (worsted) weight yarn (5 oz/ 256 yds/142g per skein): 1 skein #9700 baby pink
- Size F/5/3.75mm crochet hook or size needed to obtain gauge
- Tapestry needle
- Sewing needle
- 1 yd ¼-inch wide white ribbon
- Matching sewing thread

Sunshine Afghan

Design by *Christine Grazioso-Moody*

Finished Size
47 inches x 47 inches

Materials
• Lion Brand Pound of
Love medium (worsted)
weight yarn (16 oz/
1,020 yds/448g per skein):
    1 skein each #106
    pastel blue and
    #157 pastel yellow
• Size N/13/9mm crochet
hook or size needed to
obtain gauge
• Tapestry needle

Gauge

With 2 strands of yarn held tog: 4 V-sts = 4¾ inches; 5 rows = 4¾ inches

Pattern Notes

Weave in ends as work progresses.

Join with slip stitch as indicated unless otherwise stated.

Chain-3 at beginning of rows counts as first double crochet unless otherwise stated.

Chain-5 at beginning of rounds counts as first double crochet and chain-2 space unless otherwise stated.

Special Stitch

V-stitch (V-st): 2 dc in indicated place.

Afghan

Row 1 (RS): With 2 strands of blue, ch 76, **V-st** *(see Special Stitch)* in 5th ch from hook, sk next ch, [V-st in next ch, sk next ch] 3 times, *drop 1 strand of blue, pick up 1 strand of yellow, [V-st in next ch, sk next ch] 4 times, drop yellow, pick up new strand of blue, [V-st in next ch, sk next ch] 4 times, rep from * 3 times, dc in last ch, turn.

Row 2: Ch 3 *(see Pattern Notes)*, [V-st in sp between 2 dc of next V-st] 4 times, *drop 1 strand of blue, pick up 1 strand of yellow,

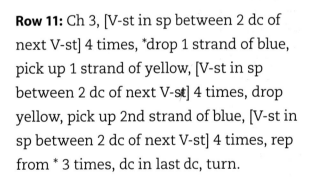

[V-st in sp between 2 dc of next V-st] 4 times, drop yellow, pick up 2nd strand of blue, [V-st in sp between 2 dc of next V-st] 4 times, rep from * 3 times, dc in last dc, turn.

Rows 3 & 4: Rep row 2.

Row 5: Ch 3, [V-st in sp between 2 dc of next V-st] 4 times, *drop 1 strand of blue, pick up 1 strand of yellow, [V-st in sp between 2 dc of next V-st] 4 times, drop yellow, pick up 2nd strand of blue, [V-st in sp between 2 dc of next V-st] 4 times, rep from * 3 times, dc in last dc, fasten off 1 strand of blue, pick up 1 strand of yellow, turn.

Row 6: Ch 3, [V-st in sp between 2 dc of next V-st] 4 times, *drop 1 strand of blue, pick up 1 strand of yellow, [V-st in sp between 2 dc of next V-st] 4 times, drop yellow, pick up 2nd strand of blue, [V-st in sp between 2 dc of next V-st] 4 times, rep from * 3 times, dc in last dc, turn.

Rows 7–9: Rep row 6.

Row 10: Ch 3, [V-st in sp between 2 dc of next V-st] 4 times, *drop 1 strand of blue, pick up 1 strand of yellow, [V-st in sp between 2 dc of next V-st] 4 times, drop yellow, pick up 2nd strand of blue, [V-st in sp between 2 dc of next V-st] 4 times, rep from * 3 times, dc in last dc. Fasten off yellow, pick up 1 strand of blue, turn.

Row 11: Ch 3, [V-st in sp between 2 dc of next V-st] 4 times, *drop 1 strand of blue, pick up 1 strand of yellow, [V-st in sp between 2 dc of next V-st] 4 times, drop yellow, pick up 2nd strand of blue, [V-st in sp between 2 dc of next V-st] 4 times, rep from * 3 times, dc in last dc, turn.

Rows 12–41: [Rep rows 2–11 consecutively] 3 times.

Rows 42–45: Rep rows 2–5. At end of last row, fasten off all colors.

Border

Rnd 1 (RS): Join *(see Pattern Notes)* 2 strands of yellow in last st of row 45, **ch 5** *(see Pattern Notes)*, dc in same st *(beg corner)*, working across side, 2 dc in end of each row across, working across next side in unused lps of starting ch, (dc, ch 2, dc) in first lp

Continued on page 107

Lemon Drops

Designs by *Sheila Leslie*

Hat
Gauge
5 sc = 1 inch

Pattern Notes
Weave in ends as work progresses.

Join with slip stitch as indicated unless otherwise stated.

Chain-3 at beginning of rows counts as first double crochet unless otherwise stated.

Special Stitches
V-stitch (V-st): (Dc, ch 1, dc) in indicated st.

Shell: 5 dc in indicated st.

Hat
Back Panel
Row 1: Ch 16, sc in 2nd ch from hook, sc in each rem ch across, turn. *(15 sc)*

Row 2: Ch 1, sc in each sc across, turn.

Rows 3–21: Rep row 2.

Row 22: Ch 1, **sc dec** *(see Stitch Guide)* in first 2 sc, sc in each of next 11 sc, sc dec in last 2 sc, turn. *(13 sc)*

Row 23: Ch 1, sc dec in first 2 sc, sc in each of next 9 sc, sc dec in last 2 sc, turn. *(11 sc)*

Row 24: Ch 1, sc dec in first 2 sc, sc in each of next 7 sc, sc dec in last 2 sc. Fasten off. *(9 sc)*

Sides & Top

Row 1: Hold piece with RS facing, join yarn with a sc in bottom corner of row 1, work 22 sc evenly sp across Back Panel, working across row 24, 2 sc in first sc, sc in each of next 7 sc, 2 sc in last sc, work 24 sc evenly sp across next side of Back Panel, turn. *(58 sc)*

Row 2: Ch 3 *(see Pattern Notes)*, sk first sc, **V-st** *(see Special Stitches)* in next sc, sk next 3 sc, **shell** *(see Special Stitches)* in next st, [sk next 3 sc, V-st in next sc, sk next 3 sc, shell in next sc] twice, sk next 3 sc, V-st in next sc, sk next 3 sc, shell in next sc, sk next 2 sc, V-st in next sc, sk next 2 sc, shell in next sc, [sk next 3 sc, V-st in next sc, sk next 3 sc, shell in next sc] twice, sk next 3 sc, V-st in next sc, sk next sc, dc in last sc, turn. *(8 V-sts, 7 shells)*

Row 3: Ch 3, *shell in ch-1 sp of next V-st, V-st in 3rd dc of next shell, rep from * across to last V-st, shell in ch-1 sp of last V-st, dc in 3rd ch of beg ch-3, turn.

Row 4: Ch 3, *V-st in 3rd dc of next shell, shell in ch-1 sp of next V-st, rep from *

across to last shell, V-st in 3rd dc of last shell, dc in 3rd ch of beg ch-3, turn.

Rows 5–10: [Rep rows 3 and 4 alternately] 3 times.

Edging

Row 1: Ch 1, sc in each dc across, 3 sc in 3rd ch of beg ch-3, work 19 sc evenly sp across lower edge of Side, work 15 sc evenly sp across Back Panel, work 19 sc evenly sp across lower edge of next Side, **join** *(see Pattern Notes)* in beg sc, turn

Row 2: Ch 3, sk first st, hdc in next st, *ch 1, sk next st, hdc in next st, rep from * 25 times across bottom edge, leaving rem sts unworked, turn.

Row 3: Ch 1, sl st in first hdc, *ch 1, sl st in next ch, ch 1, sl st in next hdc, rep from * across to beg ch-3 of row 2, (sl st, ch 1, sl st) in 2nd ch of beg ch-3, ch 1, sl st in side of same ch, working around front edge, **ch 1, sl st in next sc, rep from ** around to last hdc of row 2, join in last hdc. Fasten off.

Finishing
Weave ribbon through row 2 of Edging around bottom of Hat.

Jacket
Gauge
5 sc = 1 inch

Pattern Notes
Weave in ends as work progresses.

Join with slip stitch as indicated unless otherwise stated.

Chain-3 at beginning of rows counts as first double crochet unless otherwise stated.

Special Stitches
V-stitch (V-st): (Dc, ch 1, dc) in indicated st.

Shell: 5 dc in indicated st.

Jacket
Body
Row 1 (RS): Ch 108, sc in 2nd ch from hook, sc in each rem ch across, turn. (107 sc)

Row 2: Ch 3 (see Pattern Notes), **V-st** (see Special Stitches) in next sc, sk next 3 sc, **shell** (see Special Stitches) in next sc, sk next 3 sc, V-st in next sc, *sk next 3 sc, shell in next sc, sk next 3 sc, V-st in next sc, rep from * across to last sc, dc in last sc, turn. (14 V-sts, 13 shells)

Row 3: Ch 3, *shell in ch-1 sp of next V-st, V-st in 3rd dc of next shell, rep from * across to last V-st, shell in ch-1 sp of last V-st, dc in 3rd ch of beg ch-3, turn. (14 shells, 13 V-sts)

Row 4: Ch 3, *V-st in 3rd dc of next shell, shell in ch-1 sp of next V-st, rep from * across to last shell, V-st in 3rd dc of last shell, dc in 3rd ch of beg ch-3, turn.

Rows 5–16: [Rep rows 3 and 4 alternately] 6 times.

Right Front Yoke
Row 17: Ch 1, sc in first dc, *sk ch-1 sps, sc in each of next 22 dc, sc in next ch-1 sp, leaving rem sts unworked, turn (24 sc)

Row 18: Ch 1, sc in each sc across, turn.

Rows 19–27: Rep row 18.

Row 28: Ch 1, sc in each of first 20 sc, [**sc dec** (see Stitch Guide) in next 2 sc] twice, turn. (22 sc)

Row 29: Ch 1, sc dec in first 2 sc, sc dec in next 2 sc, sc in each of next 18 sc, turn. (20 sc)

Row 30: Ch 1, sc in each of first 16 sc, [sc dec in next 2 sc] twice, turn. (18 sc)

Row 31: Ch 1, sc dec in first 2 sc, sc dec in next 2 sc, sc in each of next 14 sc, turn. (16 sc)

Rows 32–38: Rep row 4. At end of last row, fasten off.

Left Front Yoke

Row 17: Hold piece with WS facing, sk next 7 shells from Right Front, join yarn with a sc in ch-1 sp of next V-st, sk ch-1 sps, sc in each of next 22 dc, sc in 3rd ch of beg ch-3, turn. *(24 sc)*

Row 18: Ch 1, sc in each sc across, turn.

Rows 19–27: Rep row 18.

Row 28: Ch 1, sc dec in first 2 sc, sc dec in next 2 sc, sc in each of next 20 sc, turn. *(22 sc)*

Row 29: Ch 1, sc in each of first 18 sc, [sc dec in next 2 sc] twice, turn. *(20 sc)*

Row 30: Ch 1, sc dec in first 2 sc, sc dec in next 2 sc, sc in each of next 16 sc, turn. *(18 sc)*

Row 31: Ch 1, sc in each of first 14 sc, [sc dec in next 2 sc] twice, turn. *(16 sc)*

Rows 32–38: Rep row 4. At end of last row, fasten off.

Back

Row 17: Hold piece with WS facing, join yarn with a sc in first unworked dc from Right Front, sk ch-1 sps, sc in each dc across, turn. *(49 dc)*

Row 18: Ch 1, sc in each sc across, turn.

Rows 19–34: Rep row 18.

Right Shoulder

Row 35: Ch 1, sc in each of first 18 sc, sc dec in next 2 sc, leaving rem dc unworked, turn. *(19 sc)*

Row 36: Ch 1, sc dec in first 2 sc, sc in each of next 17 sc, turn. *(18 sc)*

Row 37: Ch 1, sc in each of next 16 sc, sc dec in next 2 sc, turn. *(17 sc)*

Row 38: Ch 1, sc dec in first 2 sc, sc in each of next 15 sc. Fasten off. *(16 sc)*

Left Shoulder

Row 35: Hold piece with RS facing, sk next 9 unworked sc from Right Front, **join** (*see Pattern Notes*) yarn in next sc, sc dec in same sc as joining and in next sc, sc in each of next 18 sc, turn. *(19 sc)*

Row 36: Ch 1, sc in each of first 17 sc, sc dec in next 2 sc, turn. *(18 sc)*

Row 37: Ch 1, sc dec in first 2 sc, sc in each of next 16 sc, turn. *(17 sc)*

Row 38: Ch 1, sc in each of first 15 sc, sc dec in next 2 sc. Fasten off. *(16 sc)*

Assembly

Sew shoulder seams.

Right Sleeve

Row 1 (RS): Join yarn with a sc in right armhole in side of row 17 of Back, work 43 sc evenly sp around armhole, sc in ch-1 sp of V-st at underarm, turn. *(45 sc)*

Continued on page 107

Hearts Delight

Design by *Donna Childs*

Finished Size
28 inches x 35 inches

Materials
• Bernat Softee Baby light (light worsted) weight yarn (5 oz/468 yds/ 140g per ball):
  3 balls #02000 white
• Size F/5/3.75mm crochet hook or size needed to obtain gauge
• Tapestry needle

Gauge
19 dc = 4 inches

Pattern Notes
Weave in ends as work progresses.

Chain-3 at beginning of rows counts as first double crochet unless otherwise stated.

Special Stitches
Block: Dc in each of next 2 indicated sts or dc in next indicated ch, dc in next st.

Mesh: Ch 1, sk next indicated st or ch, dc in next st.

Afghan
Row 1 (RS): Ch 141, dc in 4th ch from hook *(beg 3 sk chs count as dc)*, dc in each rem ch across, turn. *(139 dc)*

Row 2: Ch 3 *(see Pattern Notes)*, dc in each dc across, turn.

Row 3: Ch 3, 2 **blocks** *(see Special Stitches)*, 65 **mesh** *(see Special Stitches)*, 2 blocks. *(65 mesh, 4 blocks)*

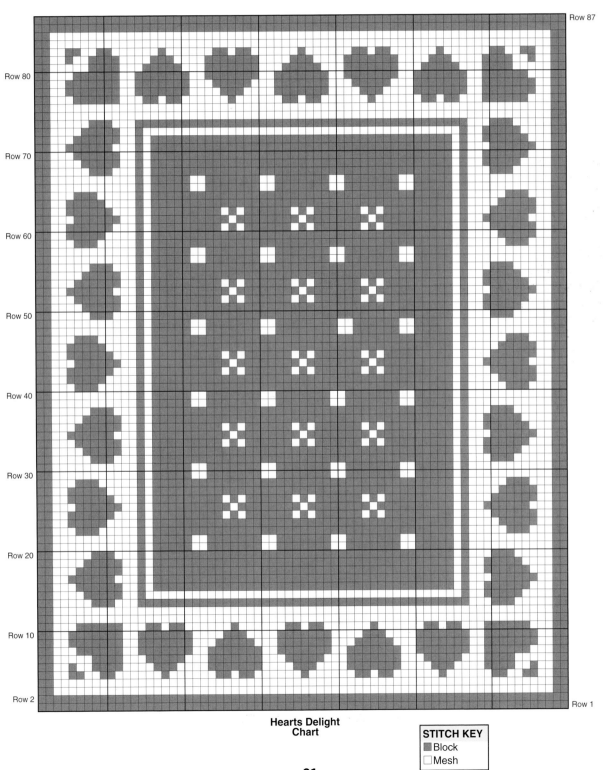

**Hearts Delight
Chart**

STITCH KEY
■ Block
□ Mesh

Rows 4–87: Using Special Stitches, work according to chart. At end of last row, fasten off.

Border

Hold piece with RS facing and row 84 at top, join yarn in first st in upper right-hand corner, ch 3, 4 dc in same st, *sk next 2 sts, sl st in next st, sk next 2 sts, 5 dc in next st, rep from * across to next corner, 7 dc in next corner, working across next side in ends of rows, sl st in next row, **5 dc in next row, sl st in next row, rep from ** across to next corner, 7 dc in corner, working across next side in unused lps of starting ch, ***5 dc in next lp, sk next 2 lps, sl st in next lp, sk next 2 lps, rep from *** across to next corner, 7 dc in corner, working across next side in ends of rows, ****5 dc in next row, sl st in next row, rep from **** across to beg ch-3, 2 dc in same st as beg ch-3, join with sl st in 3rd ch of beg ch-3. Fasten off. ●

Serenity Blue Dress

Continued from page 73

Rnd 27: Sl st in next dc, sl st in next ch-2 sp, (beg shell, ch 1, 2 dc) in same sp, ch 3, [sc in next ch-3 sp, ch 3] 4 times, (shell, ch 2, 2 dc) in ch-2 sp of next shell, ch 1, [dc in next dc, ch 1] 7 times, *(shell, ch 2, 2 dc) in ch-2 sp of next shell, ch 3, [sc in next ch-3 sp, ch 3] 4 times, (shell, ch 2, 2 dc) in ch-2 sp of next shell, ch 1, [dc in next dc, ch 1] 7 times, rep from * 7 times, join in 3rd ch of beg ch-3.

Rnd 28: Sl st in next dc, sl st in next ch-2 sp, beg shell in same sp, ch 1, shell in next ch-2 sp, ch 3, [sc in next ch-3 sp, ch 3] 3 times, shell in ch-2 sp of next shell, ch 1, shell in ch-2 sp of next shell, ch 3, [sc in next ch-1 sp, ch 3] 6 times, *shell in next ch-2 sp, ch 1, shell in next ch-2 sp, ch 3, [sc in next ch-3 sp, ch 3] 3 times, shell in ch-2 sp of next shell, ch 1, shell in ch-2 sp of next shell, ch 3, [sc in next ch-1 sp, ch 3]

6 times, rep from * 7 times, join in 3rd ch of beg ch-3.

Rnd 29: Sl st in next dc, sl st in next ch-2 sp, beg shell in same sp, ch 1, dc in next ch-1 sp, ch 1, shell in ch-2 sp of next shell, ch 3, [sc in next ch-3 sp, ch 3] twice, shell in ch-2 sp of next shell, ch 1, dc in next ch-1 sp, ch 1, shell in ch-2 sp of next shell, ch 3, [sc in next ch-3 sp, ch 3] 5 times, *shell in ch-2 sp of next shell, ch 1, dc in next ch-1 sp, ch 1, shell in ch-2 sp of next shell, ch 3, [sc in next ch-3 sp, ch 3] twice, shell in ch-2 sp of next shell, ch 1, dc in next ch-1 sp, ch 1, shell in ch-2 sp of next shell, ch 3, [sc in next ch-3 sp, ch 3] 5 times, rep from * 7 times, join in 3rd ch of beg ch-3.

Rnd 30: Sl st in next dc, sl st in next ch-2 sp, beg shell in same sp, ch 1, (dc, ch 3, dc) in next dc, ch 1, shell in ch-2 sp of next shell, ch 3, sc in next ch-3 sp, ch 3, shell in ch-2 sp of next shell, ch 1, (dc, ch 3, dc) in next dc, ch 1, shell in ch-2 sp of next shell, ch 3, [sc in next ch-3 sp, ch 3] 4 times, *shell in ch-2 sp of next shell, ch 1, (dc, ch 3, dc) in next dc, ch 1, shell in ch-2 sp of next shell, ch 3, sc in next ch-3 sp, ch 3, shell in ch-2 sp of next shell, ch 1, (dc, ch 3, dc) in next dc, ch 1, shell in ch-2 sp of next shell, ch 3, [sc in next ch-3 sp, ch 3] 4 times, rep from * 7 times, join in 3rd ch of beg ch-3.

Rnd 31: Sl st in next dc, sl st in next ch-2 sp, beg shell in same sp, ch 1, dc in next dc, 6 dc in next ch-3 sp, dc in next dc, ch 1, shell in ch-2 sp of each of next 2 shells, ch 1, dc in next dc, 6 dc in next ch-3 sp, dc in next dc, ch 1, shell in ch-2 sp of next shell, ch 3, [sc in next ch-3 sp, ch 3] 3 times, *shell in ch-2 sp of next shell, ch 1, dc in next dc, 6 dc in next ch-3 sp, dc in next dc, ch 1, shell in ch-2 sp of each of next 2 shells, ch 1, dc in next dc, 6 dc in next ch-3 sp, dc in next dc, ch 1, shell in ch-2 sp of next shell, ch 3, [sc in next ch-3 sp, ch 3] 3 times, rep from * 7 times, join in 3rd ch of beg ch-3.

Rnd 32: Sl st in next dc, sl st in next ch-2 sp, beg shell in same sp, ch 1, [dc in next dc, ch 1] 8 times, **tr dec** (*see Stitch Guide*) in ch-2 sps of next 2 shells, ch 1, dc in next dc, ch 1] 8 times, shell in ch-2 sp of next shell, ch 3,

[sc in next ch-3 sp, ch 3] twice, *shell in ch-2 sp of next shell, ch 1, [dc in next dc, ch 1] 8 times, tr dec in ch-2 sps of next 2 shells, ch 1, dc in next dc, ch 1] 8 times, shell in ch-2 sp of next shell, ch 3, [sc in next ch-3 sp, ch 3] twice, rep from * 7 times, join in 3rd ch of beg ch-3.

Rnd 33: Sl st in next dc, sl st in next ch-2 sp, beg shell in same sp, ch 2, sk next ch-1 sp, **[cl** (*see Special Stitches*) in next ch-1 sp, ch 2] 7 times, sk next ch-1 sp, cl in next st, ch 2, [cl in next ch-1 sp, ch 2] 7 times, shell in ch-2 sp of next shell, ch 3, sc in next ch-3 sp, **picot** (*see Special Stitches*), ch 3, *shell in ch-2 sp of next shell, ch 2, sk next ch-1 sp, [cl in next ch-1 sp, ch 2] 7 times, sk next ch-1 sp, cl in next st, ch 2, [cl in next ch-1 sp, ch 2] 7 times, shell in ch-2 sp of next shell, ch 3, sc in next ch-3 sp, picot, ch 3, rep from * 7 times, join in 3rd ch of beg ch-3.

Rnd 34: Sl st in next dc, sl st in next ch-2 sp, beg shell in same sp, ch 3, [dc in next cl, ch 3] 15 times, shell in ch-2 sp of next shell, ch 3, *shell in ch-2 sp of next shell, ch 3, [dc in next cl, ch 3] 15 times, shell in ch-2 sp of next shell, ch 3, rep from * 7 times, join in 3rd ch of beg ch-3.

Rnd 35: Sl st in next dc, sl st in next ch-2 sp, ch 3, cl in same sp, ch 4, [cl in next ch-3 sp, ch 4] 6 times, **lg cl** (*see Special Stitches*) in next 2 ch sps, ch 4, [cl in next ch-3 sp, ch 4] 7 times, lg cl in ch-2 sps of next 2 shells, ch 4, *[cl in next ch-3 sp, ch 4] 7 times, lg cl in next 2 ch sps, ch 4, [cl in next ch-3 sp, ch 4] 7 times, lg cl in ch-2 sps of next 2 shells, ch 4, rep from * 7 times, join in beg cl.

Rnd 36: Ch 1, sl st in next ch-4 sp, sc in same sp, picot, ch 6, *sc in next ch-4 sp, picot, ch 6, rep from * around to last ch-4 sp, sc in last ch-4 sp, join with dc in first sc.

Rnd 37: Ch 1, sl st in next ch-6 sp, sc in same sp, picot, ch 6, *sc in next ch-6 sp, picot, ch 6, rep from * around to last ch-6 sp, sc in last ch-6 sp, join with dc in first sc.

Rnd 38: Rep rnd 37. Fasten off.

Neck Edging

Rnd 1 (RS): Hold piece with RS facing, join yarn at center back at base of row 14, ch 1, work 33 sc evenly sp across left edge to starting ch of yoke, 3 sc in first ch, sc evenly sp across neck and shoulder to last ch, 3 sc in last ch, work 32 sc evenly sp across right back, join in beg sc.

Rnd 2: Ch 1, sl st in each of first 8 sc, sc in each of next 3 sc, hdc in each of next 24 sc, having last hdc in 2nd sc of 3-sc group, (sc, picot, sc) in same sc as last hdc, sc in each of next 3 sc, *(sc, picot, sc) in next sc, sc in each of next 3 sc, rep from * across to next 3-sc group, sc in first sc of 3-sc group, (2 sc, picot, sc) in next sc, ch 3, sk next 3 sc, sc in each of next 8 sc, ch 3, sk next 3 sc, sc in each of next 8 sc, ch 3, sk next 3 sc, sc in next sc, sl st in each rem sc, join in beg sl st. Fasten off.

Sleeves

Rnd 1 (RS): Hold piece with RS facing, join yarn in any sc in 1 underarm, ch 1, work 62 sc evenly sp around opening, join in beg sc. (62 sc)

Rnd 2: Ch 1, sc in same sc, ch 3, sk next sc, [sc in next sc, ch 3, sk next sc] 29 times, sc in next sc, ch 1, join with hdc in first sc. (31 ch-3 sps)

Rnd 3: Ch 1, *sc in next ch-3 sp, ch 3, rep from * around to last ch-3 sp, sc in last ch-3 sp, ch 1, join with hdc in beg sc.

Rnds 4–11: Rep rnd 3.

Rnd 12: Ch 1, 2 sc in next ch-3 sp, sc in each of next 2 ch-3 sps, [2 sc in next ch-3 sp, sc in each of next 2 ch-3 sps] 8 times, 2 sc in next ch-3 sp, sc dec in next 2 ch-3 sps, join in beg sc. (40 sc)

Rnd 13: Ch 1, sc in each sc around, join in beg sc.

Rnd 14: Rep rnd 13.

Rnd 15: Ch 2, hdc in same sc as joining, ch 1, *sk next sc, hdc in next sc, ch 1, rep from* around, sk beg ch-2 sp, join in beg hdc.

Rnd 16: Ch 1, [sc in next ch-1 sp, picot, ch 6, sk next ch-1 sp] 10 times, join in first sc. Fasten off.

Rnd 17: Working in front of rnd 16, join yarn in any sk ch-1 sp on rnd 15, ch 1, sc in same sp, picot, ch 6, working behind next picot, sc in next sk ch-1 sp on rnd 15, picot, ch 6, *working in front of next picot, sc in next sk ch-1 sp on rnd 15, picot, ch 6, working behind next picot, sc in next sk ch-1 sp on rnd 15, picot, ch 6, rep from * around, join in beg sc. Fasten off.

Finishing

Step 1: Sew buttons opposite buttonholes.

Step 2: Cut a 36-inch length of ribbon. Weave through sts of rnd 10 of Dress; tack ends to WS.

Step 3: Cut 2 lengths of ribbon, each 14 inches long. Weave 1 ribbon through rnd 15 of each Sleeve. Tack ends to WS.

Step 4: Referring to photo for placement, sew ribbon rose trim to front of Dress. ●

Boy Blue Sunday Suit

Continued from page 77

Rnd 14: Ch 3, dc in same dc as joining, dc in each of next 12 dc, ch 1, sk next dc, dc in next ch-1 sp, dc in each of next 2 dc, ch 1, sk next dc, dc in each of next 2 dc, dc in next ch-1 sp, ch 1, sk next dc, dc in each of next 14 dc, ch 1, sk next dc, dc in next ch-1 sp, dc in each of next 2 dc, ch 1, sk next dc, dc in each of next 2 dc, dc in next ch-1 sp, ch 1, sk next dc, dc in each of last 73 dc, sk beg ch-3, join in first dc.

Rnd 15: Ch 3, dc in same dc as joining, dc in each of next 12 dc, dc in next ch-1 sp, ch 1, sk next dc, dc in each of next 2 dc, dc in next ch-1 sp, dc in each of next 2 dc, ch 1, sk next dc, dc in next ch-1 sp, dc in each of next 14 dc, dc in next ch-1 sp, ch 1, sk next dc, dc in each of next 2 dc, dc in next ch-1 sp, dc in each of next 2 dc, ch 1, sk next dc, dc in next ch-1 sp, dc in each of last 73 dc, sk beg ch-3, join in first dc.

Rnd 16: Ch 3, dc in same dc as joining, dc in each of next 13 dc, dc in next ch-1 sp, ch 1, sk next dc, dc in each of next 3 dc, ch 1, sk next dc, dc in next ch-1 sp, dc in each of next 16 dc, dc in next ch-1 sp, ch 1, sk next dc, dc in each of next 3 dc, ch 1, sk next dc, dc in next ch-1 sp, dc in each of last 74 dc, sk beg ch-3, join in first dc.

Rnd 17: Ch 3, dc in same dc as joining, dc in each of next 14 dc, dc in next ch-1 sp, ch 1, sk next dc, dc in next dc, ch 1, sk next dc, dc in next ch-1 sp, dc in each of next 18 dc, dc in next ch-1 sp, ch 1, sk next dc, dc in next dc, ch 1, sk next dc, dc in next ch-1 sp, dc in each of last 75 dc, sk beg ch-3, join in first dc.

Rnd 18: Ch 3, dc in same dc as joining, dc in each of next 15 dc, dc in next ch-1 sp, ch 1, sk next dc, dc in next ch-1 sp, dc in each of next 20 dc, dc in next ch-1 sp, ch 1, sk next dc, dc in next ch-1 sp, dc in each of last 76 dc, sk beg ch-3, join in first dc.

Rnd 19: Ch 3, dc in same dc as joining, dc in each rem dc and in each ch-1 sp around, sk beg ch-3, join in first dc. *(118 dc)*

Rnd 20: Ch 3, dc in same dc as joining, dc in each rem dc around, sk beg ch-3, join in first dc.

Rnds 21 & 22: Rep rnd 20.

Waistband

Row 22: Now working in rows, ch 1, *
sc in each dc across, turn.

Row 23: Ch 1, sc in each sc across, turn.

Rows 24–29: Rep row 23.

Row 30: Fold rows 23–29 to WS over elastic, working in sc of row 29 and in sc of row 23 at same time, sl st in each sc across. Fasten off.

Bib

Row 1 (RS): Hold piece with RS facing and folded edge of Waistband at top, join yarn in same dc of rnd 21 as 14th sc of rnd 22 of Waistband made, ch 3, dc in same dc as joining, working in same dc of rnd 21 as sc of rnd 22, dc in each of next 15 dc, ch 1, sk next dc, dc in each of next 16 dc, leaving rem sts unworked, turn. *(32 dc, 1 ch-1 sp)*

Row 2: Ch 3, dc in each of first 15 dc, ch 1, sk next dc, dc in next ch-1 sp, ch 1, sk next dc, dc in each of last 15 dc, leaving beg ch-3 unworked, turn.

Row 3: Ch 3, dc in each of first 14 dc, ch 1, sk next dc, dc in next ch-1 sp, dc in next dc, dc in next ch-1 sp, ch 1, sk next dc, dc in each of last 14 dc, leaving beg ch-3 unworked, turn.

Row 4: Ch 3, dc in each of first 13 dc, ch 1, sk next dc, dc in next ch-1 sp, dc in each of next 3 dc, dc in next ch-1 sp, ch 1, sk next dc, dc in each of last 13 dc, leaving beg ch-3 unworked, turn.

Row 5: Ch 3, dc in each of first 12 dc, ch 1, sk next dc, dc in next ch-1 sp, dc in each of next 2 dc, ch 1, sk next dc, dc in each of next 2 dc, dc in next ch-1 sp, ch 1, sk next dc, dc in each of last 12 dc, leaving beg ch-3 unworked, turn.

Row 6: Ch 3, dc in each of first 12 dc, dc in next ch-1 sp, ch 1, sk next dc, dc in each of next 2 dc, dc in next ch-1 sp, dc in each of next 2 dc, ch 1, sk next dc, dc in next ch-1 sp, dc in each of last 12 dc, leaving beg ch-3 unworked, turn.

Row 7: Ch 3, dc in each of first 13 dc, dc in next ch-1 sp, ch 1, sk next dc, dc in each of next 3 dc, ch 1, sk next dc, dc in next ch-1 sp, dc in each of last 13 dc, leaving beg ch-3 unworked, turn.

Row 8: Ch 3, dc in each of first 14 dc, dc in next ch-1 sp, ch 1, sk next dc, dc in next dc, ch 1, sk next dc, dc in next ch-1 sp, dc in each of last 14 dc, leaving beg ch-3 unworked, turn.

Row 9: Ch 3, dc in each of first 15 dc, dc in next ch-1 sp, ch 1, sk next dc, dc in next ch-1 sp, dc in each of last 15 dc, leaving beg ch-3 unworked, **do not turn.**

Edging

Ch 1, 3 sc in last dc of row 9, working across side, work 18 sc evenly sp down to Waistband, working in same dc on rnd 21 as sc of rnd 22 made, sc in each of next 26 dc of rnd 21, ch 5 (*buttonhole*), sk next 5 dc, sc in each of next 23 dc, ch 5 (*buttonhole*), sk next 5 dc, sc in each of next 26 sts dc, working up side of Bib, work 18 sc evenly sp across to first dc of row 9, working across row 9, 3 sc in first dc, sc in each dc and in each ch-1 sp across to beg sc, join in beg sc, turn.

Right Strap

Row 1 (WS): Ch 1, sl st in each of first 3 sc, ch 1, sc in same sc as last sl st made, sc in each of next 4 sc, leaving rem sc unworked, turn. (*5 sc*)

Row 2 (RS): Ch 1, sc in each sc across, turn.

Rows 3–63: Rep row 2.

Row 64: Ch 1, sc dec in first 2 sc, sc in next sc, sc dec in last 2 sc, turn. (*3 sc*)

Row 65: Ch 1, sc dec in 3 sc. Fasten off.

Left Strap

Row 1 (WS): Hold Bib with WS facing, join yarn on Edging in 19th sc from Right Strap, ch 1, sc in same sc as joining, sc in each of next 4 sc, leaving rem sts unworked, turn. (*5 sc*)

Rows 2–65: Rep rows 2–65 of Right Strap.

Finishing

Sew 1 button to each Strap approximately 1–1½ inches from end of last row. Referring to photo for placement, sew 1 button to Waistband on each side of Bib.

Jacket

Body

Row 1 (RS): Ch 132, dc in 4th ch from hook, dc in each rem ch across, turn. (*129 dc*)

Row 2: Ch 3, dc in each of first 16 dc, ch 1, sk next dc, dc in each of next 47 dc, ch 1, sk next dc, dc in each of next 47 dc, ch 1, sk next dc, dc in each of last 16 dc, leaving beg ch-3 unworked, turn.

Row 3: Ch 3, dc in each of first 15 dc, *ch 1, sk next dc, dc in next ch-1 sp, ch 1, sk next dc, dc in each of next 45 dc, rep from * once, ch 1, sk next dc, dc in next ch-1 sp, ch 1, sk next dc, dc in each of last 15 dc, leaving beg ch-3 unworked, turn.

Row 4: Ch 3, dc in each of first 14 dc, *ch 1, sk next dc, dc in next ch-1 sp, dc in next dc, dc in next ch-1 sp, ch 1, sk next dc, dc in each of next 43 dc, rep from * once, ch 1, sk next dc, dc in next ch-1 sp, dc in next dc, dc in next ch-1 sp, ch 1, sk next dc, dc in each of last 14 dc, leaving beg ch-3 unworked, turn.

Row 5: Ch 3, dc in each of first 13 dc, *ch 1, sk next dc, dc in next ch-1 sp, dc in each of next 3 dc, dc in next ch-1 sp, ch 1, sk next dc, dc in each of next 41 dc, rep from * once, ch 1, sk next dc, dc in next ch-1 sp, dc in each of next 3 dc, dc in next ch-1 sp, ch 1, sk next dc, dc in each of last 13 dc, leaving beg ch-3 unworked, turn.

Row 6: Ch 3, dc in each of first 12 dc, *ch 1, sk next dc, dc in next ch-1 sp, dc in each of next 2 dc, ch 1, sk next dc, dc in each of next 2 dc, dc in next ch-1 sp, ch 1, sk next dc, dc in each of next 39 dc, rep from * once, ch 1, sk next dc, dc in next ch-1 sp, dc in each of next 2 dc, ch 1, sk next dc, dc in each of next 2 dc, dc in next ch-1 sp, ch 1, sk next dc, dc in each of last 12 dc, leaving beg ch-3 unworked, turn.

Row 7: Ch 3, dc in each of first 12 dc, *dc in next ch-1 sp, ch 1, sk next dc, dc in each of next 2 dc, dc in next ch-1 sp, dc in each of next 2 dc, ch 1, sk next dc, dc in each of next 39 dc, rep from * once, dc in next ch-1 sp, ch 1, sk next dc, dc in each of next 2 dc, dc in next ch-1 sp, dc in each of next 2 dc, ch 1, sk next dc, dc in each of last 12 dc, leaving beg ch-3 unworked, turn.

Row 8: Ch 3, dc in each of first 13 dc, *dc in next ch-1 sp, ch 1, sk next dc, dc in each of next 3 dc, ch 1, sk next dc, dc in next ch-1

sp, dc in each of next 41 dc, rep from * once, dc in next ch-1 sp, ch 1, sk next dc, dc in each of next 3 dc, ch 1, sk next dc, dc in next ch-1 sp, dc in each of last 13 dc, leaving beg ch-3 unworked, turn.

Row 9: Ch 3, dc in each of first 14 dc, *dc in next ch-1 sp, ch 1, sk next dc, dc in next dc, ch 1, sk next dc, dc in next ch-1 sp, dc in each of next 43 dc, rep from * once, dc in next ch-1 sp, ch 1, sk next dc, dc in next dc, ch 1, sk next dc, dc in next ch-1 sp, dc in each of last 14 dc, sk beg ch-3, leaving beg ch-3 unworked, turn.

Row 10: Ch 3, dc in each of first 15 dc, *dc in next ch-1 sp, ch 1, sk next dc, dc in next ch-1 sp, dc in each of next 45 dc, rep from * once, dc in next ch-1 sp, ch 1, sk next dc, dc in next ch-1 sp, dc in each of last 15 dc, sk beg ch-3, leaving beg ch-3 unworked, turn.

Row 11: Ch 3, dc in each dc across, sk beg ch-3, leaving beg ch-3 unworked, turn.

Rows 12–20: Rep rows 2–10.

Row 21: Rep row 11.

Left Front

Row 22: Ch 3, **dc dec** *(see Stitch Guide)* in first 2 dc, dc in each of next 14 dc, ch 1, sk next dc, dc in each of next 13 dc, leaving rem dc unworked, turn.

Note: *Mark 5th dc from last dc made on previous row.*

Row 23: Ch 3, dc in each of first 12 dc, ch 1, sk next dc, dc in next ch-1 sp, ch 1, sk next dc, dc in each of next 12 dc, dc dec in last 2 dc, leaving beg ch-3 unworked, turn.

Row 24: Ch 3, dc dec in first 2 dc, dc in each of next 10 dc, ch 1, sk next dc, dc in next ch-1 sp, dc in next dc, dc in next ch-1 sp, ch 1, sk next dc, dc in each of last 11 dc, leaving beg ch-3 unworked, turn.

Row 25: Ch 3, dc in each of first 10 dc, ch 1, sk next dc, dc in next ch-1 sp, dc in each of next 3 dc, dc in next ch-1 sp, ch 1, sk next dc, dc in each of next 8 dc, dc dec in last 2 dc, leaving beg ch-3 unworked, turn.

Row 26: Ch 3, dc dec in first 2 dc, dc in each of next 6 dc, ch 1, sk next dc, dc in next ch-1 sp, dc in each of next 2 dc, ch 1, sk next dc, dc in each of next 2 dc, dc in next ch-1 sp, ch 1, sk next dc, dc in each of last 9 dc, leaving beg ch-3 unworked, turn.

Row 27: Ch 3, dc in each of first 9 dc, dc in next ch-1 sp, ch 1, sk next dc, dc in each of next 2 dc, dc in next ch-1 sp, dc in each of next 2 dc, ch 1, sk next dc, dc in each of next 5 dc, dc dec in last 2 dc, leaving beg ch-3 unworked, turn.

Row 28: Ch 3, dc dec in first 2 dc, dc in each of next 5 dc, dc in next ch-1 sp, ch 1, sk next dc, dc in each of next 3 dc, ch 1, sk next dc, dc in next ch-1 sp, dc in each of last 10 dc, leaving beg ch-3 unworked, turn.

Row 29: Ch 3, dc in each of first 11 dc, dc in next ch-1 sp, ch 1, sk next dc, dc in next dc, ch 1, sk next dc, dc in next ch-1 sp, dc in each of next 5 dc, dc dec in last 2 dc, leaving beg ch-3 unworked, turn.

Row 30: Ch 3, dc dec in first 2 dc, dc in each of next 5 dc, dc in next ch-1 sp, ch 1, sk next dc, dc in next ch-1 sp, dc in each of last 12 dc, leaving beg ch-3 unworked, turn.

Row 31: Ch 3, dc in each dc and in each ch-1 sp across to last 2 dc, dc dec in last 2 dc. Fasten off.

Right Front

Row 22 (WS): Hold piece with WS facing, join yarn in 30th dc from end of row 21, ch 3, dc in same dc as joining, dc in each of next 12 dc, ch 1, sk next dc, dc in each of next 14 dc, dc dec in last 2 dc, turn.

Row 23 (RS): Ch 3, dc dec in first 2 dc, dc in each of next 12 dc, ch 1, sk next dc, dc in next ch-1 sp, ch 1, sk next dc, dc in each of last 12 dc, leaving beg ch-3 unworked, turn.

Row 24: Ch 3, dc in each of first 11 dc, ch 1, sk next dc, dc in next ch-1 sp, dc in next dc, dc in next ch-1 sp, ch 1, sk next dc, dc in each of next 10 dc, dc dec in last 2 dc, leaving beg ch-3 unworked, turn.

Row 25: Ch 3, dc dec in first 2 dc, dc in each of next 8 dc, ch 1, sk next dc, dc in next ch-1 sp, dc in each of next 3 dc, dc in next ch-1 sp, ch 1, sk next dc, dc in each of last 10 dc, leaving beg ch-3 unworked, turn.

Row 26: Ch 3, dc in each of first 9 dc, ch 1, sk next dc, dc in next ch-1 sp, dc in each of next 2 dc, ch 1, sk next dc, dc in each of next 2 dc, dc in next ch-1 sp, ch 1, sk next dc, dc in each of next 6 dc, dc dec in last 2 dc, leaving beg ch-3 unworked, turn.

Row 27: Ch 3, dc dec in first 2 dc, dc in each of next 5 dc, dc in next ch-1 sp, ch 1, sk next dc, dc in each of next 2 dc, dc in next ch-1 sp, dc in each of next 2 dc, ch 1, sk next dc, dc in each of last 9 dc, leaving beg ch-3 unworked, turn.

Row 28: Ch 3, dc in each of first 9 dc, dc in next ch-1 sp, ch 1, sk next dc, dc in each of next 3 dc, ch 1, sk next dc, dc in next ch-1 sp, dc in each of next 5 dc, dc dec in last 2 dc, leaving beg ch-3 unworked, turn.

Row 29: Ch 3, dc dec in first 2 dc, dc in each of next 5 dc, dc in next ch-1 sp, ch 1, sk next dc, dc in next dc, ch 1, sk next dc, dc in next ch-1 sp, dc in each of last 11 dc, leaving beg ch-3 unworked, turn.

Row 30: Ch 3, dc in each of first 12 dc, dc in next ch-1 sp, ch 1, sk next dc, dc in next ch-1 sp, dc in each of next 5 dc, dc dec in last 2 dc, leaving beg ch-3 unworked, turn.

Row 31: Ch 3, dc dec in first 2 dc, dc in each rem dc and in each ch-1 sp across. Fasten off.

Back

Row 22 (WS): Hold piece with WS facing, join yarn in marked dc on row 21, ch 3, dc in same dc, dc in each of next 29 dc, ch 1, sk next dc, dc in each of next 30 dc, leaving rem 4 sts unworked, turn.

Row 23: Ch 3, dc in each of first 29 dc, ch 1, sk next dc, dc in next ch-1 sp, ch 1, sk next dc, dc in each of last 29 dc, leaving beg ch-3 unworked, turn.

Row 24: Ch 3, dc in each of first 28 dc, ch 1, sk next dc, dc in next ch-1 sp, dc in next dc, dc in next ch-1 sp, ch 1, sk next dc, dc in each of last 28 dc, leaving beg ch-3 unworked, turn.

Row 25: Ch 3, dc in each of first 27 dc, ch 1, sk next dc, dc in next ch-1 sp, dc in each of next 3 dc, dc in next ch-1 sp, ch 1, sk next dc, dc in each of last 27 dc, leaving beg ch-3 unworked, turn.

Row 26: Ch 3, dc in each of first 12 dc, ch 1, sk next dc, dc in next ch-1 sp, dc in each of next 2 dc, ch 1, sk next dc, dc in each of next 2 dc, dc in next ch-1 sp, ch 1, sk next dc, dc in each of last 26 dc, leaving beg ch-3 unworked, turn.

Row 27: Ch 3, dc in each of first 26 dc, dc in next ch-1 sp, ch 1, sk next dc, dc in each of next 2 dc, dc in next ch-1 sp, dc in each of next 2 dc, ch 1, sk next dc, dc in each of last 26 dc, leaving beg ch-3 unworked, turn.

Row 28: Ch 3, dc in each of first 27 dc, dc in next ch-1 sp, ch 1, sk next dc, dc in each of next 3 dc, ch 1, sk next dc, dc in next ch-1 sp, dc in each of last 27 dc, leaving beg ch-3 unworked, turn.

Row 29: Ch 3, dc in each of first 28 dc, dc in next ch-1 sp, ch 1, sk next dc, dc in next dc, ch 1, sk next dc, dc in next ch-1 sp, dc in each of last 28 dc, leaving beg ch-3 unworked, turn.

Row 30: Ch 3, dc in each of first 29 dc, dc in next ch-1 sp, ch 1, sk next dc, dc in next ch-1 sp, dc in each of last 29 dc, leaving beg ch-3 unworked, turn.

Row 31: Ch 3, dc in each dc and in each ch-1 sp across, leaving beg ch-3 unworked, turn. (*20 dc*)

Row 32: Hold WS of Left Front facing WS of Back, matching sts, working through both thicknesses at same time, sl st in each of next 20 dc. Fasten off.

Hold WS of Right Front facing WS of Back matching first 20 dc of row 31 of Back to row 31 of Right Front, working through both thicknesses at same time, join yarn in first dc, sl st in each of next 19 dc. Fasten off.

Right Sleeve

Rnd 1: Hold Back with RS facing, join yarn in 3rd sk dc of right underarm section, ch 1, sc in same dc as joining, sc in next sk dc, work 41 sc evenly sp around armhole to first 2 sk dc of underarm section, sc in each of next 2 sk dc, **join** (*see Pattern Notes*) in beg sc. (*45 sc*)

Rnd 2: Ch 3, dc in same sc as joining, dc in each rem sc, join in first dc.

Rnd 3: Ch 3, dc in same dc as joining, dc in each of next 21 dc, ch 1, sk next dc, dc in each of next 22 dc, sk beg ch-3, join in first dc.

Rnd 3: Ch 3, dc in each of first 21 dc, ch 1, sk next dc, dc in next ch-1 sp, ch 1, sk next dc, dc in each of last 21 dc, sk beg ch-3, join in first dc.

Rnd 4: Ch 3, dc in each of first 20 dc, ch 1, sk next dc, dc in next ch-1 sp, dc in next dc, dc in next ch-1 sp, ch 1, sk next dc, dc in each of last 20 dc, sk beg ch-3, join in first dc.

Rnd 5: Ch 3, dc in each of first 19 dc, ch 1, sk next dc, dc in next ch-1 sp, dc in each of next 3 dc, dc in next ch-1 sp, ch 1, sk next dc, dc in each of last 19 dc, sk beg ch-3, join in first dc.

Rnd 6: Ch 3, dc in each of first 18 dc, ch 1, sk next dc, dc in next ch-1 sp, dc in each of next 2 dc, ch 1, sk next dc, dc in each of next 2 dc, dc in next ch-1 sp, ch 1, sk next dc, dc in each of last 18 dc, sk beg ch-3, join in first dc.

Rnd 7: Ch 3, dc in each of first 18 dc, dc in next ch-1 sp, ch 1, sk next dc, dc in each of next 2 dc, dc in next ch-1 sp, dc in each of next 2 dc, ch 1, sk next dc, dc in each of last 18 dc, sk beg ch-3, join in first dc.

Rnd 8: Ch 3, dc in each of first 19 dc, dc in next ch-1 sp, ch 1, sk next dc, dc in each of next 3 dc, ch 1, sk next dc, dc in next ch-1 sp, dc in each of last 19 dc, sk beg ch-3, join in first dc.

Rnd 9: Ch 3, dc in each of first 20 dc, dc in next ch-1 sp, ch 1, sk next dc, dc in next dc, ch 1, sk next dc, dc in next ch-1 sp, dc in each of last 20 dc, sk beg ch-3, join in first dc.

Rnd 10: Ch 3, dc in each of first 21 dc, dc in next ch-1 sp, ch 1, sk next dc, dc in next ch-1 sp, dc in each of last 21 dc, sk beg ch-3, join in first dc.

Rnd 11: Ch 3, dc in same dc as joining, dc in each rem dc and in each ch-1 sp around, sk beg ch-3, join in first dc.

Rnd 12: Ch 3, dc in same dc as joining, dc in each rem dc around, sk beg ch-3, join in first dc.

Rnds 13–16: Rep rnd 12.

Rnd 17: Ch 1, sc in same dc as joining, sc around, working **sc dec** *(see Stitch Guide)* 5 times evenly sp, join in beg sc. *(40 sc)*

Rnd 18: Ch 1, sc in same sc as joining, sc around, working sc dec 5 times evenly sp, join in beg sc. *(35 sc)*

Rnd 19: Ch 1, sc in same sc as joining, sc around, working sc dec 5 times evenly sp, join in beg sc. *(30 sc)*

Rnd 20: Ch 1, sc in same sc as joining, sc in each rem sc, join in beg sc.

Rnd 21: Ch 1, sc in each sc around, join in beg sc. Fasten off.

Left Sleeve
Work Left Sleeve in same manner in left armhole opening.

Edging
Rnd 1 (RS): Hold piece with RS facing and Right Front edge at top, join yarn in last ch of starting ch of Right Front, ch 1, (2 sc, hdc) in same ch as joining, work 41 hdc evenly sp across Right Front edge to end of row 21, (hdc, 2 sc) in first dc on row 21, work 20 sc evenly sp to shoulder seam, sc in shoulder seam, sc in each st around neck edge to next shoulder seam, sc in shoulder seam, work 20 sc evenly sp to last dc on row 21, (2 sc, hdc) in last dc, work 41 sc evenly sp across Right Front edge to row 1, 3 sc in first unused lp of starting ch of Right Front, working in sp between **posts** *(see Stitch Guide)* of dc on row 1, sc in each sp across to beg sc, join in beg sc.

Rnd 2: Ch 1, sc in same sc as joining, 3 sc in next sc, sc in each st to 2nd sc of next 3-st group, 3 sc in 2nd sc, sc in each st to st before first sc of next 3-st group, sc in st before first sc of 3-st group, ch 5 *(buttonhole)*, sk next 3 sc, [sc in each of next 7 sc, ch 5 *(buttonhole)*, sk next 5 sc] 3 times, sc in each of next 6 sc, join in beg sc. Fasten off.

Rnd 3: Hold piece with RS facing, join yarn in first sc of first 3-sc group made on rnd 2, working left to right, ch 1, **reverse sc** *(see Fig. 1)* in each sc across bottom edge to 3rd sc of next 3-sc group, sl st in 3rd sc of next 3-sc group. Fasten off.

Finishing

Sew buttons opposite buttonholes. ●

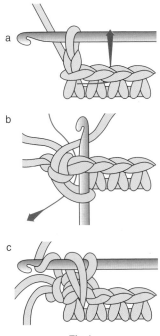

Fig 1.
Reverse Single Crochet

Baby Boy Sheriff
Continued from page 79

Row 2: Ch 3, dc in each dc across, turn.

Rows 3–8 [3–10, 3–12]: Rep row 2.

Neck Shaping

Row 1 (RS): Ch 1, sc in each of first 2 [3, 3] dc, dc in each of next 19 [19, 20] dc, turn.

Row 2: Ch 3, dc in each of first 15 [15, 16] sts, sc in each of next 3 sts, turn.

Row 3: Ch 1, sc in each of first 3 sc, dc in each of next 15 [15, 16] sts, turn.

Size 3 Months Only

Row 4: Rep row 2. Fasten off.

Size 6 Months Only

Rows [4 & 5]: Rep rows 2 and 3. At end of last row, fasten off.

12 Months Only

Rows [4 & 5]: Rep rows 2 and 3.

Row [6]: Rep row 2. Fasten off.

Assembly

Sew shoulder seams.

Sleeve

Rnd 1 (RS): Starting at underarm, join MC in 1 underarm, ch 3, work 36 [38, 40] dc evenly sp around armhole, **join** *(see Pattern Notes)* in 3rd ch of beg ch-3, turn. *(37 [39, 41] dc)*

Rnd 2: Ch 3, dc in each dc around to last dc, sk last dc, join in 3rd ch of beg ch-3, turn. *(36 [38, 40] dc)*

Rnds 3–10 [3–12, 3–14]: Rep rnd 2. *(28 [28, 28 dc] at end of last rnd)*

Cuff

Rnd 1: Ch 3, dc in next dc, **dc dec** *(see Stitch Guide)* in next 2 dc, dc dec in next 2 dc, [dc in next dc, dc dec in next 2 dc] 3 times, join in 3rd ch of beg ch-3, turn.

Rnd 2: Ch 3, dc in each dc across, join in 3rd ch of beg ch-3. Fasten off. *(19 [19, 19] dc)*

Edging

Hold Cuff with RS facing, join A in first dc, ch 1, sc in each dc around, join in beg sc. Fasten off.

Hood

Row 1: Hold piece with WS facing, join MC in first st of left neck edge, ch 3, work 15 [17, 20] dc across edge to shoulder seam, work 18 [20, 20] dc evenly sp across back neck edge to next shoulder seam, work 16 [18, 20] dc evenly sp across right neck edge, turn. *(52 [56, 60] dc)*

Row 2: Ch 3, dc in each dc across, turn.

Rows 3–15 [3–17, 3–19]: Rep row 2.

Row 16 [18, 20]: Ch 3, dc in each of next 14 [15, 16] dc, sc in each of next 3 [4, 5] dc, sl st in each of next 18 dc, sc in each of next 3 [4, 5] dc, dc in each of next 14 [15, 16] dc, turn.

Row 17 [19, 21]: Flatten piece, ch 1, working through both thicknesses at same time, sc in each dc across. Fasten off.

Edging

Row 1: Hold piece with RS facing and Right Front edge at top, join A in end of row 1, ch 1, 2 sc in same sp, working in ends of rows across Right Front edge, work 2 sc in each row, working around neckline, work sc in each sc, working in ends of rows across Left Front edge, work 2 sc in each row to row 1, **change color** *(see Stitch Guide)* to CC in last sc, turn.

Row 2: Ch 2, sc in each of first 3 sc, *pc *(see Special Stitch)* in next sc, sc in each of next 3 sc, rep from * across, change color to A in last sc, turn.

Row 3: Ch 1, sc in each of first 7 sts, *pc in next sc, sc in each of next 3 sts, rep from * across. Fasten off.

Neck Ties

Hold piece with RS facing, join MC in top corner of Right Front, ch 40 [50, 50]. Fasten off. Work Tie in top corner of Left Front in same manner.

Star

Rnd 1 (RS): With A, ch 3, join with sl st in first ch to form a ring, ch 3, 4 dc in ring, join in 3rd ch of beg ch-3.

Rnd 2: *Ch 7, sc in 4th ch from hook, hdc in next ch, dc in next ch, tr in next ch, sk next 2 dc, sc in next dc, rep from *

4 times. Leaving 8-inch end for sewing, fasten off.

Fringe

Cut 32 lengths of MC, each 4 inches long. For each knot of fringe, fold 2 strands in half. From RS, draw folded end through 1 st on underarm of 1 Sleeve. Draw ends through

fold and tighten knot. Place 7 knots evenly spaced across underarm. Repeat placing 8 knots on 2nd Sleeve. Trim ends even.

Finishing

Referring to photo for placement and with 8-inch end left for sewing, sew Star to Left Front. ●

Sunday Pink

Continued from page 83

Chain-3 at beginning of rounds counts as first double crochet unless otherwise stated.

Chain-5 at beginning of rounds counts as first double crochet and chain-2 space unless otherwise stated.

Special Stitches

Beginning cluster (beg cl): Ch 3, keeping back last lp of each dc, 2 dc in indicated sp, yo and draw through all 3 lps on hook.

Cluster (cl): Keeping back last lp of each dc, 3 dc in indicated st, yo and draw through all 4 lps on hook.

Picot: Ch 3, sl st in last st made.

Purse

Rnd 1 (RS): Ch 3, **join** (*see Pattern Notes*) in first ch to form a ring, **ch 3** (*see Pattern Notes*), 16 dc in ring, join in 3rd ch of beg ch-3. (*17 dc*)

Rnd 2: Ch 3, dc in same ch as joining, 2 dc in each dc around, join in 3rd ch of beg ch-3. (*34 dc*)

Rnd 3: Ch 3, dc in same ch as joining, 2 dc in next dc, *dc in next dc, 2 dc in each of next 2 dc, rep from * around to last 2 dc, dc in each of last 2 dc, join in 3rd ch of beg ch-3. (*56 dc*)

Rnd 4: Ch 3, dc in each of next 3 dc, *2 dc in next dc, dc in each of next 4 dc, rep from * around to last 2 dc, 2 dc in next dc, dc in last dc, join in 3rd ch of beg ch-3. (*67 dc*)

Rnd 5: Ch 3, dc in each of next 7 dc, *2 dc in next dc, dc in each of next 4 dc, rep from * around to last 2 dc, 2 dc in next dc, dc in last dc, join in 3rd ch of beg ch-3. (*78 dc*)

105

Rnd 6: Ch 3, dc in each of next 11 dc, *dc dec (*see Stitch Guide*) in next 2 dc, dc in each of next 12 dc, rep from * 3 times, dc dec in next 2 dc, dc in each of next 6 dc, dc dec in last 2 dc, join in 3rd ch of beg ch-3. *(72 dc)*

Rnd 7: Ch 3, dc in each dc around, join in 3rd ch of beg ch-3.

Rnds 8 & 9: Rep rnd 7.

Rnd 10: Ch 1, sc in each dc around, join in beg sc.

Border

Rnd 11: Ch 3, sk next 5 sc, *(dc, ch 1, dc, ch 3, dc, ch 1, dc) in next sc, sk next 5 sc, rep from * 10 times, (dc, ch 1, dc, ch 3, dc, ch 1) in same sc as beg ch-3, join in 3rd ch of beg ch-3.

Rnd 12: Sl st in next dc, sl st in next ch-1 sp, sl st in next ch-3 sp, (**beg cl**—*see Special Stitches*, ch 3, **cl**—*see Special Stitches*) in same sp, ch 3, *(cl, ch 3, cl) in next ch-3 sp, ch 3, rep from * around, join in top of beg cl.

Rnd 13: Sl st in next ch-3 sp, beg cl in same sp, ch 2, dc in next ch-3 sp, ch 2, *cl in next ch-3 sp, ch 2, dc in next ch-3 sp, ch 2, rep from * around, join in top of beg cl.

Rnd 14: Ch 5 (*see Pattern Notes*), (dc, ch 1, dc) in next dc, ch 2, *dc in next cl, ch 2, (dc, ch 1, dc) in next dc, ch 2, rep from * around, join in 3rd ch of beg ch-5.

Rnd 15: Ch 1, sc in same ch as joining, ch 3, *dc in next ch-1 sp, ch 3, sk next dc, sc in next dc, ch 3, rep from * around, join in beg sc.

Rnd 16: Ch 1, sc in same sc as joining, ch 1, (hdc, ch 1, dc) in next ch-3 sp, ch 1, (dc, **picot**—*see Special Stitches*, dc) in next dc, ch 1, (dc, ch 1, hdc) in next ch-3 sp, ch 1, *sc in next sc, ch 1, (hdc, ch 1, dc) in next ch-3 sp, ch 1, (dc, picot, dc) in next dc, ch 1, (dc, ch 1, hdc) in next ch-3 sp, ch 1, rep from * around, join in beg sc. Fasten off.

Handle

Row 1 (RS): Ch 7, dc in 4th ch from hook (*beg 3 sk chs count as a dc*), dc in each of next 3 chs, turn. *(5 dc)*

Row 2: Ch 3, dc in each of next 4 dc, turn.

Rows 3–19: Rep row 2. At end of last row, fasten off.

Finishing

Cut a 25-inch length of ribbon. Weave ribbon through ch-1 sps of rnd 14. Gather slightly and tie in a bow. Sew ends of Handle to sides of Purse. ●

Sunshine Afghan
Continued from page 85

(corner), dc in each unused lp across to last lp, (dc, ch 2, dc) in last lp (corner), working across next side in ends of rows, 2 dc in each row across, working across row 45, (dc, ch 2, dc) in first st (corner), dc in each st across to beg ch-5, join in 3rd ch of beg ch-5. Fasten off.

Rnd 2: Join 2 strands of blue in any corner ch-2 sp, ch 1, 4 sc in same sp (corner), *sc in each dc across to next corner ch-2 sp, 4 sc in corner ch-2 sp (corner), rep from * twice, sc in each dc across to beg sc, join in beg sc. Fasten off. ●

Lemon Drops
Continued from page 89

Row 2: Ch 3, sk next 3 sts, V-st in next sc, sk next 3 sc, shell in next sc, *sk next 3 sc, V-st in next sc, sk next 3 sc, shell in next sc, rep from * 3 times, sk next 3 sc, V-st in next sc, dc in last sc, turn. (6 V-sts, 5 shells)

Row 3: Ch 3, *shell in ch-1 sp of next V-st, V-st in 3rd dc of next shell, rep from * across to last V-st, shell in ch-1 sp of last V-st, dc in 3rd ch of beg ch-3, turn.

Row 4: Ch 3, *V-st in 3rd dc of next shell, shell in ch-1 sp of next V-st, rep from * across to last shell, V-st in 3rd dc of last shell, dc in 3rd ch of beg ch-3, turn.

Rows 5–14: [Rep rows 3 and 4 alternately] 5 times.

Row 15: Ch 1, sc in each dc across, sc in 3rd ch of beg ch-3, turn. (39 sc)

Row 16: Ch 1, sc in first sc, sc dec in next 2 sc, *sc in next sc, sc dec in next 2 sc, rep from * across, turn. (26 sc)

Row 17: Ch 1, sc in each sc across, turn.

Row 18: Rep row 17.

Row 19: Ch 1, sl st in first sc, *ch 1, sl st in next sc, rep from * across. Fasten off.

Left Sleeve
Work in same manner as Right Sleeve, joining yarn with a sc in left armhole in side of row 17 of Back.

Assembly
Sew Sleeve seams.

Edging

Rnd 1: Hold piece with WS facing and Left Front edge at top, join yarn with a sc at bottom corner of Left Front, work 30 sc evenly sp up front to yoke, work 11 sc evenly sp up yoke to neck shaping, 2 sc in each of next 3 sts around curve, work 8 sc evenly sp to shoulder seam, work 4 sc evenly sp down left back neck edge, sc in each of 9 sk sts of Back, work 4 sc evenly sp across right back neck edge, work 8 sc evenly sp around to curve, 2 sc in each of 3 sts around curve, work 11 sc evenly sp down yoke, work 30 sc evenly sp down Right Front edge, 3 sc in bottom corner, work 105 sc evenly sp across bottom edge, 2 sc in same place as beg sc, join in beg sc, turn. *(238 sc)*

Rnd 2: Ch 1, (sl st, ch 1, sl st) in first sc, *ch 1, sl st in next sc, rep from * around lower edge to 2nd sc of 3-sc group at Right Front corner, (sl st, ch 1, sl st) in 2nd sc, **ch 1, sl st in next sc, rep from ** to first sc of next 2-sc group at yoke, sl st in first sc, ch 3, sk next sc, sl st in next sc, ***ch 1, sl st in next sc, rep from *** to last sc of last 2-sc group at Left Front yoke, sl st in first sc, ch 3, sk next sc, sl st in next sc, ****ch 1, sl st in next sc, rep from **** to beg sl st, join in beg sl st. Fasten off.

Finishing

Cut 2 lengths of ribbon, each 14 inches long. Thread 1 length through 1 ch-3 sp made on row 2 of Edging at front neck. Fold end over ½ inch and tack in place. Rep with rem length in rem ch-3 sp.

Booties
Gauge

5 sc = 1 inch

Pattern Notes

Weave in ends as work progresses.

Join with slip stitch as indicated unless otherwise stated.

Chain-3 at beginning of rounds counts as first double crochet unless otherwise stated.

Special Stitches

Beginning V-stitch (beg V-st): Ch 4, dc in indicated st.

V-stitch (V-st): (Dc, ch 1, dc) in indicated st.

Beginning shell (beg shell): Ch 3, 4 dc in indicated st.

Shell: 5 dc in indicated st.

Bootie

Make 2.

Note: *Piece is worked in continuous rounds. Do not join unless specified; mark beginning of rounds.*

Rnd 1: Ch 12, 2 sc in 2nd ch from hook, sc in each of next 6 chs, hdc in each of next 3 chs, 5 hdc in last ch, working in unused

---

Materials
Booties
• Bernat Softee Baby light (light worsted) weight yarn (5 oz/468 yds/ 140g per ball):
  1 ball #02003 lemon
• Size F/5/3.75mm crochet hook or size needed to obtain gauge
• Tapestry needle
• Sewing needle
• 1 yd ¼-inch wide ribbon
• Matching sewing thread

lps on opposite side of starting ch, hdc in each of next 3 lps, sc in each of next 7 lps, 2 sc in last lp. *(28 sts)*

Rnd 2: Sc in next sc, 2 sc in next sc, sc in each of next 6 sts, hdc in each of next 5 sts, 2 hdc in each of next 3 sts, hdc in each of next 4 sts, sc in each of next 6 sts, 2 sc in next st, sc in next st. *(33 sc)*

Rnd 3: Sc in each of next 2 sts, 2 sc in next st, sc in each of next 8 sts, hdc in each of next 3 sts, [2 hdc in next st, hdc in next st] 3 times, hdc in each of next 3 sts, sc in each of next 8 sts, 2 sc in next st, sc in next st. *(38 sts)*

Rnd 4: Sc in next st, 2 sc in next st, sc in each of next 15 sts, [2 sc in next st, sc in next st] 3 times, sc in each of next 12 sts, 2 sc in next st, sc in each of next 2 sts. *(43 sc)*

Rnd 5: Sc in each sc around.

Rnd 6: Rep rnd 5.

Rnd 7: Sc in each of next 18 sc, [dc dec *(see Stitch Guide)* in next 2 sc] 5 times, sc in each of next 15 sc. *(38 sts)*

Rnd 8: Sc dec *(see Stitch Guide)* in next 2 sts, sc in each of next 16 sts, [dc dec in next 2 sts] 3 times, sc in each of next 14 sts. *(34 sts)*

Rnd 9: Sc in each of next 17 sts, [dc dec in next 2 sts] twice, sc in each of next 13 sts. *(32 sts)*

Rnd 10: Sc in each of next 16 sts, [dc dec in next 2 sts] twice, sc in each of next 12 sts. *(30 sts)*

Rnd 11: Sc in each of next 15 sts, [dc dec in next 2 sts] twice, sc in each of next 11 sts. *(28 sts)*

Rnd 12: Sl st in next st, **ch 3** *(see Pattern Notes)*, sk next st, hdc in next st, *ch 1, sk next st, hdc in next st, rep from * around, ch 1, sk next st, join in 2nd ch of beg ch-3. *(14 ch-1 sps)*

Rnd 13: Beg V-st *(see Special Stitches)* in same ch as joining, sk next hdc, **shell** *(see Special Stitches)* in next hdc, sk next ch-1 sp, **V-st** *(see Special Stitches)* in next sp, sk next ch-1 sp, shell in next ch-1 sp, sk next hdc, V-st in next hdc, sk next hdc, shell in next hdc, sk next ch-1 sp, V-st in next ch-1 sp, sk next ch-1 sp, shell in next ch-1 sp, join in 3rd ch of beg ch-4. *(4 shells, 4 V-sts)*

Rnd 14: Sl st in next ch-1 sp, **beg shell** *(see Special Stitches)* in same sp, V-st in 3rd dc of next shell, *shell in ch-1 sp of next V-st, V-st in 3rd dc of next shell, rep from * around, join in 3rd ch of beg ch-3.

Rnd 15: Sl st in each of next 2 dc, beg V-st in last dc and last sl st, shell in ch-1 sp of next V st, *V-st in 3rd dc of next shell, shell in ch-1 sp of next V-st, rep from * around, join in 3rd ch of beg ch-4. Fasten off.

Finishing
Cut 2 lengths of ribbon, each 18 inches long. Starting at front, thread 1 length through rnd 12 of each bootie. Tie each ribbon in bow. ●

Just for Fun

These projects are guaranteed to put a smile on your face. Make them for a friend or just because they are so much fun. Everyone is sure to want one!

Funky Hat

Design by *Darla Sims*

Skill Level

EASY

Finished Size

21 inches in
circumference

Materials

• Red Heart Super Saver
medium (worsted) weight
yarn (solids: 7 oz/
364 yds/198g per skein;
prints: 5 oz/244 yds/
141g per skein):
  1 skein each
    #512 turqua and
    #784 bonbon print
  1 yd #312 black
• Sizes H/8/5mm and
I/9/5.5mm crochet
hooks or size needed
to obtain gauge
• Tapestry needle

Gauge

Size I hook: 6 hdc =
2 inches

Pattern Notes

Weave in ends as work
progresses.

Join with slip stitch
as indicated unless
otherwise stated.

Chain-3 at beginning of
rounds counts as first
double crochet unless
otherwise stated.

Special Stitch

Curl: Ch 7, 2 sc in 2nd
ch from hook, 2 sc in
each of next 5 chs.

Hat

Rnd 1 (RS): Beg at bottom with size I hook and turqua, ch 60,
join (see Pattern Notes) in first ch to form a ring, **ch 3** (see Pattern
Notes), dc in each ch around, join in 3rd ch of beg ch-3. (60 dc)

Rnd 2: Ch 3, dc in each dc around, join in 3rd ch of beg ch-3. Change color to bonbon print by drawing lp through, drop turqua.

Rnd 3: Ch 1, sc in same ch as joining, *curl (*see Special Stitch*), sc in each of next 4 dc, rep from * around to last 3 dc, curl, sc in each of last 3 dc, join in beg sc. Change to turqua, drop bonbon print.

Rnd 4: Ch 3, dc in each sc around, join in 3rd ch of beg ch-3.

Rnd 5: Ch 3, dc in each dc around, join in 3rd ch of beg ch-3. Change to bonbon print by drawing lp through, drop turqua.

Rnd 6: Ch 1, sc in same ch as joining, sc in each of next 2 dc, *curl, sc in each of next 4 dc, rep from * around to last dc, curl, sc in last dc, join in beg sc. Change to turqua, drop bonbon print.

Rnds 7 & 8: Rep rnds 4 and 5.

Rnd 9: Ch 1, sc in same sc as joining, sc in next dc, *curl, sc in each of next 4 dc, rep from * around to last 2 dc, curl, sc in each of last 2 dc, join in beg sc. Change to turqua, drop bonbon print.

Rnds 10 & 11: Rep rnds 4 and 5.

Rnd 12: Ch 1, sc in same sc as joining, *curl, sc in each of next 4 dc, rep from * around to last 3 dc, curl, sc in each of last 3 dc, join in beg sc. Change to turqua, fasten off bonbon print.

Rnd 13: Ch 1, sc in same sc as joining, sc in each sc around, join in beg sc.

Rnd 14: Ch 1, **sc dec** (*see Stitch Guide*) in first 2 sc, *sc dec in next 2 sc, rep from * around, join in beg sc. (*30 sc*)

Rnd 15: Ch 3, dc in each sc around, join in 3rd ch of beg ch-3.

Rnd 16: Ch 3, dc in each dc around, join in 3rd ch of beg ch-3.

Rnd 17: Rep rnd 16. Fasten off.

First Ear Flap

Row 1 (RS): Hold Hat with RS facing and beg ch at top, with size I hook, join turqua with sc in any unused lp of beg ch-60, working in unused lps of beg ch, sk next 2 lps, 5 dc in next lp, sk next 2 lps, sc in next lp, leaving rem lps unworked, turn. (*7 sts*)

Row 2: Ch 2, sc in first sc, hdc in next dc, 2 dc in each of next 3 dc, hdc in next dc, sc in next sc, sl st in next unused lp of beg ch-60, turn. (*11 sts, 1 ch-2 sp*)

Row 3: Sk first sl st, sc in each of next 10 sts, sc in 2nd ch of beg ch-2, sl st in next unused lp of beg ch-60. Fasten off. (*12 sts*)

Tie

With size I hook, join bonbon print to center st of row 3, ch 45, 2 sc in 2nd ch from hook, sc in each of next 7 chs, sl st in each rem ch across, sl st in same st as joining. Fasten off.

Continued on page 124

Bath Mitts

Designs by *Darla Sims*

Finished Sizes

Lion: 7 inches at widest part x 8 inches
Elephant: 7 inches at widest part x 8 inches

Materials

Lion
• Lily Sugar'n Cream medium (worsted) weight cotton yarn (2½ oz/ 120 yds/70g per ball):
  2 balls each
   #00010 yellow and
   #01628 hot orange
• Medium (worsted) weight cotton yarn:
  1 yd black
• Size H/8/5mm crochet hook or size needed to obtain gauge
• Tapestry needle
• Stitch marker

Elephant
• Lily Sugar'n Cream medium (worsted) weight cotton yarn (solids: 2½ oz/120 yds/70g per ball; ombres: 2 oz/ 95 yds/56g per ball):
  3 balls #02744
   swimming pool
  2 balls #00001 white
• Medium (worsted) weight cotton yarn:
  1 yd black
• Size H/8/5mm crochet hook or size needed to obtain gauge
• Tapestry needle

Lion

Gauge

13 sc = 4 inches

Pattern Notes

Weave in ends as work progresses.

Join with slip stitch as indicated unless otherwise stated.

Mitt

Body

Make 2.

Row 1 (RS): With yellow, ch 17, sc in 2nd ch from hook, sc in each rem ch across, turn. *(16 sc)*

Row 2: Ch 1, sc in each sc across, turn.

Rows 3–10: Rep row 2.

Row 11: Ch 1, 2 sc in first sc, sc in each sc to last sc, 2 sc in last sc, turn. *(18 sc)*

Rows 12 & 13: Rep row 11. *(22 sc at end of last row)*

Rows 14–17: Rep row 2.

Row 18: Ch 1, **sc dec** *(see Stitch Guide)* in next 3 sc, sc in each sc to last 3 sts, sc dec in last 3 sc turn. *(18 sc)*

Row 19: Rep row 18. *(14 sc at end of row)*

Row 20: Ch 1, sc dec in first 2 sc, sc in each of next 10 sc, sc dec in last 2 sc, turn. (*12 sc*)

Rows 21–23: Rep row 2.

Row 24: Ch 1, sc dec in first 2 sc, sc in each sc to last 2 sc, sc dec in last 2 sc, turn. (*10 sc*)

Rows 25 & 26: Rep row 24. At end of last row, fasten off. (*6 sc at end of last row*)

Head

Note: Head is worked in continuous rounds. Do not join unless specified; mark beg of rounds.

Rnd 1 (RS): With yellow, ch 2, 8 sc in 2nd ch from hook. (*8 sc*)

Rnd 2: 2 sc in each sc around. (*16 sc*)

Rnd 3: [Sc in next sc, 2 sc in next sc] 8 times. (*24 sc*)

Rnd 4: [Sc in each of next 2 sc, 2 sc in next sc] 8 times. (*32 sc*)

Rnd 5: [Sc in each of next 3 sc, 2 sc in next sc] 8 times, **join** (*see Pattern Notes*) in next sc. Fasten off. (*40 sc*)

Mane

Join hot orange with sc in any sc on rnd 5, ch 3, *sc in next sc, ch 3, rep from * around, join in beg sc. Fasten off.

Assembly

With black and using **satin stitch** (*Fig. 1*), embroider eyes and nose. With black and using **backstitch** (*Fig. 2*), embroider smile.

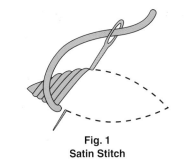

Fig. 1
Satin Stitch

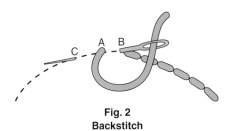

Fig. 2
Backstitch

Continued on page 124

115

Santa Toilet Seat Cover

Design by *Darla Sims*

Finished Size

Instructions given fit standard-size toilet seat

Materials

- Red Heart Light & Lofty super bulky (super chunky) weight yarn (6 oz/140 yds/170g per skein):
    1 skein #9316 puff
- Red Heart Super Saver medium (worsted) weight yarn (7 oz/364 yds/198g per skein):
    1 skein each
      #390 hot red and
      #724 baby pink
- Medium (worsted) weight yarn:
    12 inches black
- Size L/11/8mm crochet hook or size needed to obtain gauge
- Tapestry needle
- Sewing needle
- 2 black ⅝-inch buttons
- ¼ yd ⅜-inch green satin ribbon
- Matching sewing thread

Gauge

4 hdc = 2 inches

Pattern Notes

Weave in ends as work progresses.

Join with slip stitch as indicated unless otherwise stated.

Chain-2 at beginning of rows counts as first half double crochet unless otherwise stated.

Roll approximately 20 yards of puff in a separate ball. Divide baby pink in half. Holding 2 strands together, roll in a ball. Divide hot red in half. Holding 2 strands together, roll in a ball. Both baby pink and hot red are worked holding 2 strands tog.

Seat Cover

Face

Row 1 (RS): With puff, ch 12, hdc in 3rd ch from hook *(beg 2 sk chs count as a hdc)*, hdc in each rem ch across, turn. *(11 hdc)*

116

Row 2: Ch 1, 2 hdc in first hdc, hdc in each of next 9 hdc, 2 hdc in 2nd ch of beg 2 sk chs, turn. *(13 hdc)*

Row 3: Ch 1, 3 hdc in first hdc, hdc in each of next 11 hdc, 3 hdc in last hdc, turn. *(17 hdc)*

Row 4: Ch 1, 2 hdc in first hdc, hdc in each of next 15 hdc, 2 hdc in last hdc, turn. *(19 hdc)*

Row 5: Ch 2 *(see Pattern Notes)*, hdc in each hdc across, turn. *(19 hdc)*

Row 6: Ch 1, 2 hdc in first hdc, hdc in each of next 17 hdc, 2 hdc in 2nd ch of beg ch-2, turn. *(21 hdc)*

Row 7: Ch 1, 2 hdc in first hdc, hdc in each of next 17 hdc, 2 hdc in last hdc, turn. *(23 hdc)*

Row 8: Ch 2, hdc in each hdc across, turn.

Rows 9–16: Rep row 8.

Row 17: Ch 2, hdc in each of next 6 hdc, **change color** *(see Stitch Guide)* to baby pink in last hdc, hdc in each of next 9 hdc, change color to separate ball of puff in last hdc, hdc in each of next 7 hdc, turn.

Row 17: Ch 2, hdc in each of next 6 hdc, change to baby pink in last hdc, hdc in each of next 9 hdc, change to puff in last hdc, hdc in each of next 7 hdc, turn.

Row 18: Rep row 17.

Row 19: Ch 2, hdc in each of next 7 hdc, change to baby pink in last hdc, hdc in each of next 7 hdc, change to puff in last hdc, hdc in each of next 8 hdc, turn.

Rows 20 & 21: Rep row 19.

Row 22: Ch 1, **hdc dec** *(see Stitch Guide)* in first 2 hdc, hdc in each of next 5 hdc, change to baby pink in last dc, cut puff, hdc in each of next 5 hdc, change to puff in last hdc, cut baby pink, hdc in each of next 6 hdc, hdc dec in last 2 hdc, turn. *(21 hdc)*

Hat

Row 23: Ch 2, hdc in each hdc across, turn.

Row 24: Ch 2, hdc in each hdc across, change to hot red in last hdc, turn. Fasten off puff.

Row 25: Ch 1, hdc dec in first 2 hdc, hdc in each of next 17 hdc, hdc dec in next 2 hdc, turn. *(19 hdc)*

Row 26: Ch 2, hdc in each hdc across, turn.

Row 27: Ch 1, hdc dec in first 2 hdc, hdc in each of next 15 hdc, hdc dec in last 2 hdc. Fasten off. *(17 hdc)*

Top Section

Note: Piece is worked in continuous rounds. Do not join unless specified; mark beg of rnds.

Rnd 1 (RS): Beg at bottom edge, with hot red, ch 15, **join** *(see Pattern Notes)* in first ch to form a ring, ch 1, sc in same ch as joining, sc in each rem ch around. *(15 sc)*

Rnd 2: Ch 1, sc in each sc around.

Rnd 3: [Sc in next sc, sc dec in next 2 sc] 5 times. *(10 sc)*

Rnd 4: Sc in each sc around.

Rnd 5: Rep rnd 4.

Rnd 6: Sc in first sc, [sc dec in next 2 sc, sc in next sc] 3 times. (7 sc)

Rnd 7: Sc in first sc, [sc dec in next 2 sc, sc in next sc] twice. Fasten off. (3 sc)

Pompom

With puff, ch 4, 6 dc in 4th ch from hook (*beg 3 sk chs count as a dc*), **join** (*see Pattern Notes*) in 3rd ch of beg 3 sk chs. Leaving a 12-inch end, fasten off.

Eyebrow
Make 2.

With puff, ch 4, sl st in 2nd ch from hook, sc in each of next 3 chs. Fasten off.

Moustache
Make 2.

With puff, ch 5, sc in 2nd ch from hook, sc in next ch, hdc in each of last 2 chs. Fasten off.

Hat Brim

Hold Face upside down with RS facing, join puff with sc from front to back to front around **post** (*see Stitch Guide*) of first st on row 23 of Face, *ch 2, sc around post of next hdc, rep from * across. Fasten off.

Edging

Rnd 1 (RS): Join puff with sc in end of row 1 of Face, working around outer edge, sc evenly sp around and work 2 sc in each corner, join in beg sc.

Rnd 2: Ch 2, hdc in each sc around, join in 2nd ch of beg ch-2. Fasten off.

Drawstring

With 1 strand of hot red, make a chain to fit around cover, plus a few inches to allow to draw up and tie tog. Fasten off.

Finishing

Step 1: With tapestry needle, weave end of Pompom through sc of rnd 7 of Top Section. Gather sc together and secure end. Referring to photo for placement, sew Top Section to Hat.

Step 2: Tie green satin ribbon into bow; sew to Hat.

Step 3: Sew buttons to Face for eyes. Sew Moustache below eyes. With baby pink and using **lazy daisy stitch** (*Fig. 1*), embroider mouth.

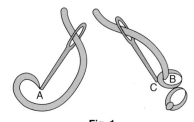

Fig. 1
Lazy Daisy Stitch

Step 4: Weave Drawstring through last rnd of Seat Cover Edging. ●

1·2·3 Skein Crochet

Checkers Game

Design by Rhonda Dodds

Gauge

4 sc = 1 inches; 3 dc = 1 inch

Pattern Notes

Weave in ends as work progresses.

Join with slip stitch as indicated unless otherwise stated.

Chain-3 at beginning of rows counts as first double crochet unless otherwise stated.

When changing colors on checkerboard strips, leave 10-inch ends for sewing on left side of each strip after changing colors.

Skill Level

■■□□
EASY

Finished Sizes

Checkerboard: 16½ inches x 16½ inches
Checker Cozy: 10½ inches x 20½ inches without handles

Materials

• Red Heart Super Saver medium (worsted) weight yarn (7 oz/364 yds/ 198g per skein):
  1 skein each
   #358 lavender and
   #254 pumpkin
• Size H/8/5mm crochet hook or size needed to obtain gauge
• Tapestry needle
• Sewing needle
• 2 wooden 5½-inch purse handles
• 3 decorative 1⅝-inch buttons
• 24 decorative ½-inch flower-shaped buttons
• Matching sewing thread
• Stitch markers

Checkerboard

Strip A

Make 4.

Row 1 (RS): With lavender, ch 8, sc in 2nd ch from hook, sc in each rem ch across, turn. *(7 sc)*

Row 2: Ch 1, sc in each sc across, turn.

Rows 3–6: Rep row 2.

Row 7: Ch 1, sc in each sc across, **change color** *(see Stitch Guide)* to pumpkin in last sc, turn.

Rows 8–13: Rep row 2.

Row 14: Ch 1, sc in each sc across, change color to lavender in last sc, turn.

Rows 15–49: [Rep rows 8–14 consecutively] 5 times.

Rows 50–55: Rep rows 8–13.

Row 56: Ch 1, sc in each sc across. Fasten off.

Strip B

Make 4.

Row 1 (RS): With pumpkin, ch 8, sc in 2nd ch from hook, sc in each rem ch across, turn. *(7 sc)*

Row 2: Ch 1, sc in each sc across, turn.

Rows 3–6: Rep row 2.

Row 7: Ch 1, sc in each sc across, change color to lavender in last sc, turn.

Rows 8–13: Rep row 2.

Row 14: Ch 1, sc in each sc across, change color to pumpkin in last sc, turn.

Rows 15–49: [Rep rows 8–14 consecutively] 5 times.

Rows 50–55: Rep rows 8–13.

Row 56: Ch 1, sc in each sc across. Fasten off.

Assembly

Referring to Assembly Diagram for placement, with RS tog and with ends left for sewing, sew Strips together, changing colors for each square.

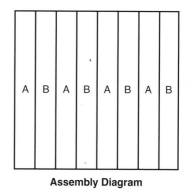

Assembly Diagram

Border

Rnd 1 (RS): Join *(see Pattern Notes)* pumpkin in any corner, ch 1, 3 sc in same sp, *working across side, sc evenly sp to next corner, 3 sc in corner, rep from * twice, working across next side, sc evenly sp across to beg sc, join in beg sc. Fasten off.

Rnd 2: Join lavender in any sc, ch 1, sc in same sc, *ch 3, sk next sc, sc in next sc, rep from * to beg sc, join in beg sc. Fasten off.

Checkers

Make 12 of each pumpkin and lavender.

Ch 4, join in first ch to form a ring, **ch 3** (*see Pattern Notes*), 14 dc in ring, leaving a 6-inch end, fasten off.

Finishing

On each Checker, bring end to front of Checker, thread 1 button on end. With tapestry needle, sew button to center of Checker. Secure end.

Checker Cozy

Row 1: With lavender, make lp on hook, working over bottom of handle, work 30 sc across handle, turn. (*30 sc*)

Row 2: Ch 3 (*see Pattern Notes*), dc in each sc across, turn.

Row 3: Ch 3, dc in each dc across, turn.

Row 4: Rep row 3.

Row 5: Ch 3, dc in first dc, dc in each dc across to last dc, 2 dc in last dc, turn. (*32 dc*)

Row 6: Rep row 5. (*34 dc at end of row*)

Rows 7–23: Rep row 3.

Row 24: Ch 3, **dc dec** (*see Stitch Guide*) in next 2 dc, dc in each of next 28 dc, dc dec in next 2 dc, dc in last dc, turn. (*32 dc*)

Row 25: Ch 3, dc dec in next 2 dc, dc in each of next 26 dc, dc dec in next 2 dc, dc in last dc, turn. (*30 dc*)

Rows 26 & 27: Rep row 3.

Row 28: Hold 2nd handle behind row 27 and working over bottom of handle, sc in each dc across. Fasten off. (*30 sc*)

Pocket

Row 1 (RS): With pumpkin, ch 31, dc in 4th ch from hook (*beg 3 sk chs count as a dc*), dc in each rem ch across, turn. (*29 dc*)

Row 2: Ch 3, dc in each dc across, turn.

Rows 3–8: Rep row 2.

Row 9: Ch 3, dc in each of next 2 dc, ch 2 (*button lp*), sk next dc, dc in each of next 10 dc, ch 2 (*button lp*), sk next dc, dc in each of next 10 dc, ch 2 (*button lp*), sk next dc, dc in each of last 3 dc. Fasten off.

Assembly

Fold Cozy in half. Referring to photo for placement, sew Pocket to front of Cozy.

Finishing

With tapestry needle and lavender, sew buttons to Cozy opposite button lps. ●

121

Colorful Dolls

Design by Donna Childs

Finished Size

9 inches tall

Materials

• Medium (worsted) weight yarn:
  5 yds each white, black, violet, raspberry, watermelon, orange, yellow, lime, blue, rose
• Size G/6/4mm crochet hook or size needed to obtain gauge
• Tapestry needle
• Polyester fiberfill

Gauge

16 sc = 4 inches

Pattern Notes

Weave in ends as work progresses.

Join with slip stitch as indicated unless otherwise stated.

Use any color desired for Doll's Head, Arms and Legs. Use 2 contrasting colors for Body.

Doll

Make 5.

Head

Rnd 1 (RS): With MC, ch 4, **join** (see Pattern Notes) in first ch to form a ring, 6 sc in ring, join in beg sc. (6 sc)

Rnd 2: Ch 1, 2 sc in ea sc around, join in beg sc. (12 sc)

Rnd 3: Ch 1, [2 sc in first sc, sc in next sc] 6 times, join in beg sc. *(18 sc)*

Rnd 4: Ch 1, [2 sc in first sc, sc in each of next 2 sc] 6 times, join in beg sc. *(24 sc)*

Rnd 5: Ch 1, sc in each sc around, join in beg sc.

Rnds 6–9: Rep rnd 5.

Rnd 10: Ch 1, [**sc dec** *(see Stitch Guide)* in first 2 sc, sc in each of next 2 sc] 6 times, join in beg sc. *(18 sc)*

Rnds 11 & 12: Rep rnd 5.

Rnd 13: Ch 1, sc dec in first 2 sc, sc in next sc, [sc dec in next 2 sc, sc in next sc] 5 times. Leaving 8-inch end for sewing, fasten off. *(12 sc)*

Arm

Make 2.

Rnd 1 (RS): With MC, ch 4, join in first ch to form a ring, 6 sc in ring, join in beg sc. *(6 sc)*

Rnd 2: Ch 1, 2 sc in each sc around, join in beg sc. *(12 sc)*

Rnd 3: Ch 1, sc in each sc around, join in beg sc.

Rnds 4–12: Rep rnd 3. At end of last rnd, leaving 8-inch end for sewing, fasten off.

Leg

Make 2.

Rnd 1 (RS): With MC, ch 4, join in first ch to form a ring, 6 sc in ring, join in beg sc. *(6 sc)*

Rnd 2: Ch 1, 2 sc in each sc around, join in beg sc. *(12 sc)*

Rnd 3: Ch 1, sc in each sc around, join in beg sc.

Rnds 4–15: Rep rnd 3. At end of last rnd, leaving 8-inch end for sewing, fasten off.

Body

Make 2.

Row 1 (RS): With A, ch 13, sc in 2nd ch from hook, sc in each rem ch across, turn. *(12 sc)*

Row 2: Ch 1, sc in each sc across, **changing color** *(see Stitch Guide)* to B in last sc, turn.

Row 3: Ch 1, sc in each sc across, turn.

Row 4: Ch 1, sc in each sc across, changing color to A in last sc, turn.

Row 5: Ch 1, sc in each sc across, turn.

Rows 6–17: [Rep rows 2–5 consecutively] 3 times.

Row 18: Ch 1, sc in each sc across. Fasten off.

Finishing

Stuff Head, Arms, and Legs with fiberfill. With MC, sew first 6 sc of Head to center 6 sc of row 18 of 1 Body piece, sew rem sc of Head to center 6 sc of 2nd Body piece. Sew rem sc of last rows of Body pieces tog to form shoulders. Sew Arms to Body flush with shoulders, sewing 6 sc of Arm to front Body piece and rem 6 sc to back Body piece. Sew Legs to bottom of Body, 6 sc of each Leg to front Body piece and rem 6 sc of each Leg to back Body piece. Sew 1 side of Body closed, lightly stuff, and sew rem side closed. ●

Funky Hat

Continued from page 113

2nd Ear Flap

Row 1 (RS): Sk next 16 unused lps of beg ch-60 from First Ear Flap, with size I hook, join turqua with sc in next unused lp, sk next 2 unused lps, 5 dc in next unused lp, sk next 2 unused lps, sc in next unused lp, leaving rem unused lps unworked, turn. *(7 sts)*

Rows 2 & 3: Rep rows 2 and 3 of First Ear Flap.

Tie

Work same as Tie for First Ear Flap.

Hat Tie

With size H hook and turqua, ch 72, sl st in 2nd ch from hook, sl st in each rem ch across. Fasten off.

Finishing

Weave Hat Tie through rnd 15 of Hat. Pull tog tightly and tie in bow. ●

Bath Mitts

Continued from page 115

Referring to photo for placement and with yellow, sew Head to 1 Body.

Hold Bodies with WS tog and beg ch to right, join yellow with sc in end of row 1, working around outer edge in ends of rows and in sc of row 26, sc in each row and in each st to opposite end of row 1. Fasten off.

Cuff

Rnd 1 (RS): Hold piece with RS facing and beg ch at top, join hot orange with sc in 1 seam, sc in each sc around, join in beg sc.

Rnd 2: Ch 1, sc in same sc and in each sc around, join in beg sc.

Rnd 3: Rep rnd 2. Fasten off.

Elephant

Gauge

13 sc = 4 inches

Pattern Notes

Weave in ends as work progresses.

Join with slip stitch as indicated unless otherwise stated.

Mitt

Body

Make 2.

Row 1 (RS): With swimming pool, ch 17, sc in 2nd ch from hook, sc in each rem ch across, turn. *(16 sc)*

Row 2: Ch 1, sc in each sc across, turn.

Rows 3–10: Rep row 2.

Row 11: Ch 1, 2 sc in first sc, sc in each sc to last sc, 2 sc in last sc, turn. *(18 sc)*

Rows 12 & 13: Rep row 11. *(22 sc at end of last row)*

Rows 14–17: Rep row 2.

Row 18: Ch 1, **sc dec** *(see Stitch Guide)* in next 3 sc, sc in each sc to last 3 sts, sc dec in last 3 sc, turn. *(18 sc)*

Row 19: Rep row 18. *(14 sc at end of row)*

Row 20: Ch 1, sc dec in first 2 sc, sc in each of next 10 sc, sc dec in last 2 sc, turn. *(12 sc)*

Rows 21–23: Rep row 2.

Row 24: Ch 1, sc dec in first 2 sc, sc in each sc to last 2 sc, sc dec in last 2 sc, turn. *(10 sc)*

Rows 25 & 26: Rep row 24. At end of last row, fasten off. *(6 sc at end of last row)*

Ear
Make 2.
Row 1 (RS): With white, ch 6, sc in 2nd ch from hook, sk next ch, 5 dc in next ch, sk next ch, sc in last ch, turn. *(7 sts)*

Row 2: Ch 1, sc in first sc, 2 sc in each of next 5 dc, sc in last sc. Fasten off. *(12 sts)*

Trunk
Row 1 (RS): With swimming pool, ch 5, sc in 2nd ch from hook, sc in each rem ch across, turn. *(4 sc)*

Row 2: Ch 1, sc in each sc across, turn.

Rows 3 & 4: Rep row 2.

Row 5: Ch 1, sc in first sc, sc dec in next 2 sc, sc in last sc, turn. *(3 sc)*

Row 6: Rep row 2.

Row 7: Ch 1, sc dec in first 2 sc, sc in last sc. Fasten off. *(2 sc)*

Assembly
With black and using **French knots** *(Fig. 1)*, embroider eyes in upper Trunk.

Fig. 1
French Knot

Referring to photo for placement, with white, sew Ears to 1 Body. With swimming pool, sew Trunk centered between Ears.

Hold Bodies with WS tog and beg ch to right; join swimming pool with sc in end of row 1, working around outer edge in ends of rows and in sc of row 26, sc in each row and in each st to opposite end of row 1. Fasten off.

Cuff
Rnd 1 (RS): Hold piece with RS facing and beg ch at top, join white with sc in seam, sc in each sc around, **join** *(see Pattern Notes)* in beg sc.

Rnd 2: Ch 1, sc in same sc and in each sc around, join in beg sc.

Rnd 3: Rep rnd 2. Fasten off. ●

Just for Home

These quick-to-stitch projects are useful
and add a touch of flair to your decor.

Pineapple Bathroom Set

Designs by *Pam Bruce*

Skill Level
■■□□
EASY

Finished Sizes
Lid Cover: 13 inches x 15 inches
Tank Cover: 23 inches

Materials
• NaturallyCaron.com Country medium (worsted) weight yarn (3 oz/185 yds/85g per ball):
  3 balls #0020 loden forest
• Size G/6/4mm crochet hook or size needed to obtain gauge
• Tapestry needle
• Sewing needle
• 28-inch piece ⅛-inch-wide elastic
• Matching sewing thread

Gauge
4 sc = 1 inch

Pattern Notes
Weave in ends as work progresses.

Join with slip stitch as indicated unless otherwise stated.

Chain-3 at beginning of rows counts as first double crochet unless otherwise stated.

Special Stitch
Shell: (2 dc, ch 2, 2 dc) in indicated st.

Large shell (lg shell): (3 dc, ch 3, 3 dc) in indicated st.

Lid Cover
Row 1 (WS): Ch 21, **shell** (*see Special Stitches*) in 6th ch from hook (*beg 5 sk chs count as 2 sk chs and a dc*), ch 2, sk next 5 chs, **lg shell** (*see Special Stitches*) in next ch, ch 2, sk next 5 chs, shell in next ch, sk next 2 chs, dc in last ch, turn. (*1 lg shell, 1 shell, 2 dc, 2 ch-2 sps*)

Row 2 (RS): Ch 3 (*see Pattern Notes*), shell in ch-2 sp of next shell, ch 2, 12 dc in ch-3 sp of next lg shell (*pineapple base*), ch 2, shell in ch-2 sp of next shell, dc in next ch of beg 5 sk chs, turn. (*2 shells, 1 lg shell, 14 dc, 2 ch-2 sps*)

Row 3: Ch 3, shell in ch-2 sp of next shell, ch 2, sk next ch-2 sp, [dc in next dc, ch 1] 11 times, dc in next dc, ch 2, shell in ch-2 sp of next shell, dc in 3rd ch of beg ch-3, turn. *(2 shells, 14 dc, 2 ch-2 sps, 11 ch-1 sps)*

Row 4: Ch 3, shell in ch-2 sp of next shell, ch 2, sk next ch-2 sp, [sc in next ch-1 sp, ch 3] 10 times, sc in next ch-1 sp, ch 2, shell in ch-2 sp of next shell, dc in 3rd ch of beg ch-3, turn. *(2 shells, 2 dc, 11 sc, 10 ch-3 sps, 2 ch-2 sps)*

Row 5: Ch 3, shell in ch-2 sp of next shell, ch 2, sk next ch-2 sp, [sc in next ch-3 sp, ch 3] 9 times, sc in next ch-3 sp, ch 2, shell in ch-2 sp of next shell, dc in 3rd ch of beg ch-3, turn. *(2 shells, 2 dc, 10 sc, 9 ch-3 sps, 2 ch-2 sps)*

Row 6: Ch 3, shell in ch-2 sp of next shell, ch 2, sk next ch-2 sp, [sc in next ch-3 sp, ch 3] 8 times, sc in next ch-3 sp, ch 2, shell in ch-2 sp of next shell, dc in 3rd ch of beg ch-3, turn. *(2 shells, 2 dc, 9 sc, 8 ch-3 sps, 2 ch-2 sps)*

Row 7: Ch 3, shell in ch-2 sp of next shell, ch 2, sk next ch-2 sp, [sc in next ch-3 sp, ch 3] 7 times, sc in next ch-3 sp, ch 2, shell in ch-2 sp of next shell, dc in 3rd ch of beg ch-3, turn. (*2 shells, 2 dc, 8 sc, 7 ch-3 sps, 2 ch-2 sps*)

Row 8: Ch 3, shell in ch-2 sp of next shell, ch 2, sk next ch-2 sp, [sc in next ch-3 sp, ch 3] 6 times, sc in next ch-3 sp, ch 2, shell in ch-2 sp of next shell, dc in 3rd ch of beg ch-3, turn. (*2 shells, 2 dc, 7 sc, 6 ch-3 sps, 2 ch-2 sps*)

Row 9: Ch 3, shell in ch-2 sp of next shell, ch 2, sk next ch-2 sp, [sc in next ch-3 sp, ch 3] 5 times, sc in next ch-3 sp, ch 2, shell in ch-2 sp of next shell, dc in 3rd ch of beg ch-3, turn. (*2 shells, 2 dc, 6 sc, 5 ch-3 sps, 2 ch-2 sps*)

Row 10: Ch 3, shell in ch-2 sp of next shell, ch 2, sk next ch-2 sp, [sc in next ch-3 sp, ch 3] 4 times, sc in next ch-3 sp, ch 2, shell in ch-2 sp of next shell, dc in 3rd ch of beg ch-3, turn. (*2 shells, 2 dc, 5 sc, 4 ch-3 sps, 2 ch-2 sps*)

Row 11: Ch 3, shell in ch-2 sp of next shell, ch 2, sk next ch-2 sp, [sc in next ch-3 sp, ch 3] 3 times, sc in next ch-3 sp, ch 2, shell in ch-2 sp of next shell, dc in 3rd ch of beg ch-3, turn. (*2 shells, 2 dc, 4 sc, 3 ch-3 sps, 2 ch-2 sps*)

Row 12: Ch 3, shell in ch-2 sp of next shell, ch 2, sk next ch-2 sp, [sc in next ch-3 sp, ch 3] twice, sc in next ch-3 sp, ch 2, shell in ch-2 sp of next shell, dc in 3rd ch of beg ch-3, turn. (*2 shells, 2 dc, 3 sc, 2 ch-3 sps, 2 ch-2 sps*)

Row 13: Ch 3, shell in ch-2 sp of next shell, ch 2, sk next ch-2 sp, sc in next ch-3 sp, ch 3, sc in next ch-3 sp, ch 2, shell in ch-2 sp of next shell, dc in 3rd ch of beg ch-3, turn. (*2 shells, 2 dc, 2 sc, 1 ch-3 sp, 2 ch-2 sps*)

Row 14: Ch 3, shell in ch-2 sp of next shell, ch 2, sk next ch-2 sp, sc in next ch-3 sp, ch 2, shell in ch-2 sp of next shell, dc in 3rd ch of beg ch-3, turn. (*2 shells, 2 dc, 1 sc, 2 ch-2 sps*)

Row 15: Ch 3, shell in ch-2 sp of next shell, tr in next sc, shell in ch-2 sp of next shell, dc in 3rd ch of beg ch-3, turn. (*2 shells, 1 tr, 2 dc*)

Edging

Rnd 1 (RS): Ch 3, sc in ch-2 sp of next shell, ch 3, sc in next tr, ch 3, sc in ch-2 sp of next shell, ch 3, working across next side, sc in sp formed by edge dc of row 15, [ch 3, sc in sp formed by edge dc of next row] 14 times, working across opposite side of starting ch, ch 3, sc in same ch as next shell on row 1 made, ch 3, sc in next ch-3 sp, ch 3, sc in same ch as next lg shell made, ch 3, sc in next ch-5 sp, ch 3, sc in same ch as next shell made, working across next side, ch 3, sc in sp formed by edge st of row 1, [ch 3, sc in sp formed by edge dc of next row] 14 times, **join** (*see Pattern Notes*) in first ch of beg ch-3. (*37 sc, 38 ch-3 sps*)

Rnd 2: Sl st in next ch of beg ch-3 of previous rnd, ch 1, sc in same sp, ch 4, [sc in next ch-3 sp, ch 4] 37 times, join in beg sc. (*38 ch-4 sps*)

Rnd 3: Sl st in each of next 2 chs of next ch-4 sp, ch 1, sc in same sp, ch 4, [sc in next ch-4 sp, ch 4] 37 times, join in beg sc.

Rnd 4: Sl st in next ch-4 sp, ch 1, 3 sc in same sp, 3 sc in each rem ch-4 sp around, join in beg sc. *(114 sc)*

Rnd 5: Ch 1, sc in each of first 5 sc, 2 sc in next sc, *sc in each of next 5 sc, 2 sc in next sc, rep from * around, join in beg sc. *(133 sc)*

Rnd 6: Ch 1, sc in each of first 3 sc, 2 sc in next sc, [sc in each of next 6 sc, 2 sc in next sc] 18 times, sc in each of next 3 sc, join in beg sc. *(152 sc)*

Rnd 7: Ch 1, sc in each of first 7 sc, 2 sc in next sc, *sc in each of next 7 sc, 2 sc in next sc, rep from * around, join in beg sc. *(171 sc)*

Rnd 8: Ch 1, sc in each of first 4 sc, 2 sc in next sc, [sc in each of next 8 sc, 2 sc in next sc] 18 times, sc in each of next 4 sc, join in beg sc. *(190 sc)*

Rnd 9: Ch 1, sc in each of first 85 sc, sl st in each of next 30 sc *(center back of lid)*, sc in each of next 75 sc, join in beg sc.

Rnd 10: Ch 1, sc in each of first 85 sc, sl st in **back lp** *(see Stitch Guide)* of each of next 30 sts, sc in each of next 75 sc, join in beg sc.

Rnd 11: Ch 1, sc in each of first 8 sc, **sc dec** *(see Stitch Guide)* in next 2 sc, [sc in each of next 8 sc, sc dec in next 2 sc] 7 times, sc in

each of next 5 sc, sl st in back lp of each of next 30 sts, sc in each of next 5 sc, [sc in each of next 8 sc, sc dec in next 2 sc] 7 times, join in beg sc. *(175 sc)*

Rnd 12: Ch 1, sc in each of first 27 sc, sl st in back lp of each of next 30 sts, sc in each of next 68 sc, join in beg sc.

Rnd 13: Ch 1, sc in each of first 7 sc, sc dec in next 2 sc, [sc in each of next 7 sc, sc dec in next 2 sc] 7 times, sc in each of next 5 sc, sl st in back lp of each of next 30 sts, sc in each of next 5 sc, [sc in each of next 7 sc, sc dec in next 2 sc] 7 times, join in beg sc. *(160 sc)*

Rnd 14: Ch 1, sc in each of first 6 sc, sc dec in next 2 sc, [sc in each of next 6 sc, sc dec in next 2 sc] 7 times, sc in each of next 5 sc, sl st in back lp of each of next 30 sts, sc in each of next 5 sc, [sc in each of next 6 sc, sc dec in next 2 sc] 7 times, join in beg sc. *(145 sc)*

Rnd 15: Sl st in each st around, join in beg sl st. Fasten off.

Tank Cover
First Half

Row 1 (RS): Ch 29, **shell** *(see Special Stitches)* in 6th ch from hook *(beg 5 sk chs count as 2 sk chs and a dc)*, ch 2, sk next 5 chs, shell in next ch, [sk next 3 chs, shell in next ch] twice, ch 2, sk next 5 chs, shell in next ch, sk next 2 chs, dc in last ch, turn. *(5 shells, 2 dc, 2 ch-2 sps)*

Continued on page 145

Delicate Lace Table Runner

Design by *Lillian Gimmelli*

Finished Size
9½ inches x 25 inches

Materials
• DMC Cebelia Crochet Cotton size 10 (1¾ oz/ 284 yds/50g per ball):
  2 balls ecru
  1 ball #223 medium dusty pink
• Size 13/.85mm steel crochet hook or size needed to obtain gauge
• Tapestry needle

Gauge
9 hdc = 1 inch; Motif = 3¼ inches x 4¼ inches

Pattern Notes
Weave in ends as work progresses.

Join with slip stitch as indicated unless otherwise stated.

Chain-3 at beginning of rows counts as first half double crochet unless otherwise stated.

Special Stitches
Beginning shell (beg shell): Ch 3, (2 dc, ch 2, 3 dc) in indicated st.

Shell: (3 dc, ch 2, 3 dc) in indicated st.

Table Runner
Motif
Make 16.

Row 1 (WS): With ecru, ch 40, hdc in 4th ch from hook (*beg 3 sk chs count as hdc*), hdc in each rem ch across, turn. (*38 hdc*)

Row 2 (RS): Ch 6, sk first 4 hdc, sl st in next hdc, [ch 6, sk next 3 hdc, sl st in next hdc] 8 times, sc in 4th ch of beg 4 sk chs, turn. (*9 ch-6 sps, 1 sc*)

Row 3: [Ch 8, sl st in next ch-6 sp] 9 times, turn. (*9 ch-8 sps*)

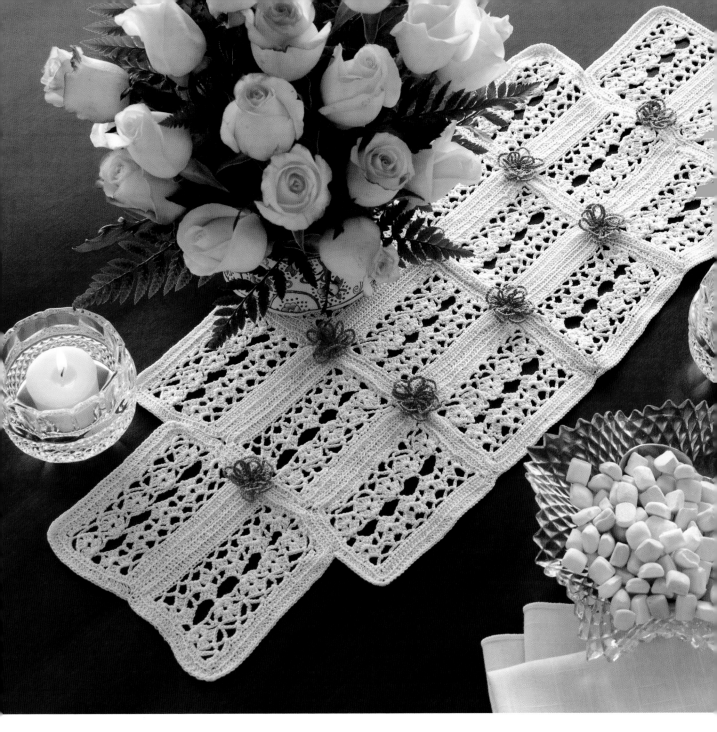

Row 4: Ch 1, sl st in first ch-8 sp, **beg shell** (*see Special Stitches*) in same sp, *ch 1, sc in next ch-8 sp, ch 1, **shell** (*see Special Stitches*) in next ch-8 sp, rep from * 3 times, turn. (*5 shells, 4 sc*)

Row 5: Ch 3 (*see Pattern Notes*), shell in ch-2 sp of next shell, *ch 2, dc in next sc, ch 2, shell in ch-2 sp of next shell, rep from * 3 times, turn. (*5 shells, 5 dc*)

Row 6: Ch 6, dc in ch-2 sp of next shell, *ch 10, dc in ch-2 sp of next shell, rep from * 3 times, ch 6, dc in 3rd ch of beg ch-3, turn. (*6 dc, 4 ch-10 sps, 2 ch-6 sps*)

Row 7: Sl st in first ch-6 sp, ch 3, shell in next dc, *ch 2, dc in next ch-10 sp, ch 2, shell in next dc, rep from * 3 times, ch 2, dc in 3rd ch of beg ch-6, turn. (*5 shells, 6 dc, 9 ch-2 sps*)

Continued on page 147

Dust Mitt

Design by *Pamela Noel*

Finished Size
11 inches x 13 inches, including fringe

Materials
• Medium (worsted) weight yarn:
   5 oz/250 yds/142g purple
   2 oz/100 yds/56g variegated
• Size G/6/4mm crochet hook or size needed to obtain gauge
• Tapestry needle

Gauge
4 sc = 1 inch

Pattern Notes
Weave in ends as work progresses.

Join with slip stitch as indicated unless otherwise stated.

Chain-2 at beginning of rounds counts as first half double crochet unless otherwise stated.

Chain-3 at beginning of rounds counts as first double crochet unless otherwise stated.

Mitt

Rnd 1 (RS): With variegated, ch 16, 3 sc in 2nd ch from hook, sc in each of next 13 chs, 3 sc in last ch, working in unused lps on opposite side of ch, sc in each of next 13 lps, **join** *(see Pattern Notes)* in beg sc. *(32 sc)*

***Note:** Through rnd 33, piece is worked in **back lps** (see Stitch Guide) and in continuous rounds. Do not join unless specified; mark beginning of rnds.*

Rnd 2: Ch 1, 2 sc in each of first 3 sc, sc in each of next 13 sc, 2 sc in each of next 3 sc, 2 sc in each of next 13 sc. *(38 sc)*

Rnd 3: *[2 sc in next sc, sc in next sc] 3 times, sc in each of next 13 sc, rep from * once. *(44 sc)*

Rnd 4: *[2 sc in next sc, sc in each of next 2 sc] 3 times, sc in each of next 13 sc, rep from * once. (50 *sc*)

Rnd 5: Sc in each sc around.

Rnds 6–29: Rep rnd 5.

Rnd 30: [Sc dec *(see Stitch Guide)* in next 2 sc, sc in each of next 2 sc] 3 times, sc in each of next 13 sc, rep from * once, join in first sc. (44 *sc*)

Rnd 31: Rep rnd 5.

Rnd 32: [Sc dec in next 2 sc, sc in next sc] 3 times, sc in each of next 13 sc, rep from * once, join in first sc. (38 *sc*)

Rnd 33: Ch 3 *(see Pattern Notes)*, dc in each sc around, join in 3rd ch of beg ch-3.

Rnd 34: Ch 2 *(see Pattern Notes)*, **fpdc** *(see Stitch Guide)* around next dc, [**bpdc** *(see Stitch Guide)* of next dc, fpdc around next dc] 18 times, join in 2nd ch of beg ch-2.

Rnd 35: Ch 2, fpdc around next st, [bpdc around next st, fpdc around next st] 18 times, join in 2nd ch of beg ch-2.

Rnd 36: Rep rnd 35.

Rnd 37: Ch 2, fpdc around next st, [bpdc around next st, fpdc around next st] 18 times, join in 2nd ch of beg ch 2, sl st

in each of next 2 sts, (sl st, ch 10, sl st) in next st *(hanging lp)*. Fasten off.

Fringe
Note: *Mark front lp of 19th sc on rnd 7 of Mitt.* Cut 6-inch strands of purple. Use 1 strand for each knot of Fringe. Fold strand in half, insert hook in **front lp** *(see Stitch Guide)* of first st on rnd 1, draw folded end through lp, draw ends through fold and tighten knot. Tie knots in rem front lps on rnd 1 and in front lps on rnds 2–6. On rnd 7, leaving front lp of marked sc and front lps of each of next 16 sc fringeless, tie knots in rem front lps of rnd. Work fringe in same manner on rnds 8–31. Trim ends even. ●

Tweed Granny Rug

Design by Katherine Eng

Skill Level
■■■□
INTERMEDIATE

Finished Size
19½ inches x 28½ inches

Materials
• TLC Essentials medium (worsted) weight yarn (solids: 6 oz/312 yds/170g per skein; multis: 4½ oz/245 yds/127g per skein):
   1 skein each #2958 falling leaves, #2919 barn red, #2936 claret
• Size I/9/5.5mm crochet hook or size needed to obtain gauge
• Tapestry needle

Gauge
Rnds 1 & 2 = 3½ inches

Pattern Notes
Weave in ends as work progresses.

Join with slip stitch as indicated unless otherwise stated.

Chain-3 at beginning of rounds counts as first double crochet unless otherwise stated.

Special Stitch
Picot: Ch 2, sl st in **front lp** *(see Stitch Guide)* of 2nd ch from hook.

Rug
First Motif

Rnd 1 (RS): With 1 strand of falling leaves and 1 strand of barn red held tog, ch 4, **join** *(see Pattern Notes)* in first ch to form a ring, **ch 3** *(see Pattern Notes)*, 2 dc in ring, ch 2, [3 dc in ring, ch 2] 3 times, join in 3rd ch of beg ch-3. Fasten off. *(12 dc, 4 ch-2 sps)*

Rnd 2: With 1 strand of barn red and 1 strand of claret held tog, join in any ch-2 sp, ch 3, (2 dc, ch 2, 3 dc) in same sp, ch 1, [(3 dc, ch 2, 3 dc) in next ch-2 sp, ch 1] 3 times, join in 3rd ch of beg ch-3. Fasten off.

Rnd 3: With 1 strand of falling leaves and 1 strand of claret held tog as 1, join in any ch-1 sp, ch 1, (sc, ch 2, sc) in same sp, *ch 2, (sc, ch 2, sc, ch 4, sc, ch 2, sc) in next ch-2 sp *(corner)*, ch 2 **, (sc, ch 2, sc) in next ch-1 sp, rep from * 3 times, ending last rep at **, join in beg sc. Fasten off.

2nd Motif

Rnds 1 & 2: Rep rnds 1 and 2 of First Motif.

Rnd 3: With 1 strand of falling leaves and 1 strand of claret held tog, join in any ch-1 sp, ch 1, (sc, ch 2, sc) in same sp, ch 2, (sc, ch 2, sc) in next ch-2 sp, ch 2, hold WS of completed Motif facing WS of working Motif, drop double-stranded lp from hook, draw lp under and over corresponding ch-4 sp on completed Motif, ch 2, (sc, ch 2, sc) in same sp on working Motif, ch 2, sc in next ch-1 sp, ch 1, drop lp from hook, draw lp under and over corresponding ch-2 sp on completed Motif, ch 1, sc in same sp on working Motif, ch 2, (sc, ch 2, sc) in next ch-2 sp, ch 2, drop lp from hook, draw lp under and over corresponding ch-4 sp on completed Motif, ch 2, (sc, ch 2, sc) in same sp on working Motif, *ch 2, (sc, ch 2, sc) in next ch-1 sp, ch 2, (sc, ch 2, sc, ch 4, sc, ch 2, sc) in next ch-2 sp *(corner)*, rep from * once, ch 2, join in beg sc. Fasten off.

Continued on page 148

Scrub a Dub

Design by *Emma Willey*

Gauge

4 V-sts & 3 ch-3 sps = 2 inches

Pattern Notes

Weave in ends as work progresses.

Chain-4 at beginning of rounds counts as first double crochet and chain-1 space unless otherwise stated.

Chain-6 at beginning of rounds counts as first double crochet and chain-3 space unless otherwise stated.

Special Stitches

Beginning V-stitch (beg V-st): Ch 4, dc in indicated sp.

V-stitch (V-st): (Dc, ch 1, dc) in indicated sp.

Holder

Row 1 (WS): Ch 53, tr in 7th ch from hook *(beg 6 sk chs count as sk ch, a tr and a ch-1 sp)*, *ch 1, sk next ch, tr in next ch, rep from * across, turn. *(25 tr, 24 ch-1 sps)*

Row 2 (RS): Sl st in next ch-1 sp, **beg V-st** *(see Special Stitches)* in same sp, ch 1, dc in next ch-1 sp, *ch 1, **V-st** *(see Special Stitches)* in next ch-1 sp, ch 1, dc in next ch-1 sp, rep from * 10 times, turn. *(12 V-sts, 12 dc, 23 ch-1 sps)*

Row 3: Ch 4 *(see Pattern Notes)*, V-st in ch-1 sp of next V-st, *ch 3, V-st in ch-1 sp of next V-st, rep from * across, turn. *(12 V-sts, 12 ch-3 sps, 1 ch-1 sp, 1 dc)*

Row 4: Sl st in next ch-1 sp, beg V-st in same sp, [ch 3, V-st in ch-1 sp of next V-st] 11 times, ch 1, dc in 3rd ch of beg ch-4. *(12 V-sts, 11 ch-3 sps, 1 ch-1 sp, 1 dc)*

Row 5: Ch 4, V-st in ch-1 sp of next V-st, *ch 3, V-st in ch-1 sp of next V-st, rep from * across, turn.

Rows 6–15: [Rep rows 4 and 5 alternately] 5 times.

Row 16: Rep row 4. At end of row, fasten off.

Edging

Row 1 (RS): Fold piece in half lengthwise and hold folded piece with row 16 at top, working through both thicknesses at same time in ch-1 sps of V-sts, join crochet cotton with sl st in first ch-1 sp in right-hand corner, **ch 6** *(see Pattern Notes)*, [dc in ch-1 sp of next V-st, ch 3] 4 times, (dc, ch 3) twice in ch-1 sp of next V-st, working across next side in ends of rows, work [dc, ch 2] 12 times evenly sp across to row 1, dc in end of row 1, turn. *(20 dc, 7 ch-3 sps, 12 ch-2 sps)*

Row 2: Ch 1, sc in each dc and in each ch across. Fasten off.

Tie

Ch 20, sc in 2nd ch from hook, sc in each rem ch across. Fasten off.

Finishing

Starting at side, weave Tie through ch-1 sps on row 1 of Holder. Knot ends together. ●

Peachy Clean

Design by *Kyleigh Hawke*

Finished Size
5 inches x 10 inches

Materials
• Medium (worsted) weight cotton yarn:
   3 oz/150 yds/85g green
• Size H/8/5mm crochet hook or size needed to obtain gauge
• Tapestry needle

Gauge

14 dc = 4 inches

Pattern Note

Weave in ends as work progresses.

Mitt

Side

Make 2.

Row 1 (RS): Ch 18, dc in 4th ch from hook (*beg 3 sk chs count as dc*), dc in each rem ch across, turn. (*16 dc*)

Row 2: Ch 1, sc in first dc, *ch 3, sk next 2 dc, sc in next dc, rep from * across, turn. (*6 sc, 5 ch-3 sps*)

Row 3: Ch 3 (*counts as first hdc and ch-1 sp*), sc in next ch-3 sp, [ch 3, sc in next ch-3 sp] 4 times, ch 1, hdc in last sc, turn. (*2 hdc, 5 sc, 4 ch-3 sps, 2 ch-1 sps*)

Row 4: Ch 1, sc in first hdc, ch 3, sk next ch-1 sp, *sc in next ch-3 sp, ch 3, rep from * across with last sc in 2nd ch of beg ch-3, turn. (*6 sc, 5 ch sps*)

Row 5: Ch 3 (*counts as first dc*), 2 dc in each ch sp and dc in each st across, turn. (*16 dc*)

Row 6: Ch 3, dc in each dc across, turn.

Rows 7–16: [Rep rows 2–6 consecutively] twice.

Rows 17–20: Rep rows 2–5.

Row 21: Sl st in each of first 2 sts, ch 3, **dc dec** *(see Stitch Guide)* in next 2 dc, dc in each dc across to last 3 dc and beg ch-3, dc dec in next 2 dc, dc in next dc, leaving beg ch-3 unworked, turn. *(12 dc)*

Row 22: Sl st in each of next 2 sts, ch 3, dc dec in next 2 dc, dc in each dc across to last 3 dc and beg ch-3, dc dec in next 2 dc, dc in next dc, leaving beg ch-3 unworked. Fasten off. *(8 dc)*

Edging

Hold Sides with WS facing and starting ch to right, working through both thicknesses at same time, join yarn with sc in end of row 1, sc in same row, working across side in ends of rows, work 2 sc in end of each dc row and sc in end of each sc row to row 22, sc in each st across row 22, working across next side in ends of rows, work 2 sc in end of each dc row and sc in end of each sc row to row 1, 2 sc in end of row 1. Fasten off. ●

141

Apple Tea Cozy & Coasters

Designs by *Lisa Marchand Harris*

Skill Level

EASY

Finished Size
Tea Cozy: 8 inches tall, excluding Stem and Leaves
Coasters: 4 x 5¼ inches, including Stem and Leaf

Materials
Tea Cozy
• Red Heart Super Saver medium (worsted) weight yarn (7 oz/364 yds/198g per skein):
  2 oz/100 yds/56g #332 ranch red
  20 yds #368 paddy green
  ¼ yd #365 coffee
• Size H/8/5mm crochet hook or size needed to obtain gauge
• Tapestry needle
Coasters
• Red Heart Super Saver medium (worsted) weight yarn (7 oz/364 yds/ 198g per skein):
  1 oz/50 yds/28g #332 ranch red
  ¼ yd each #368 paddy green and #365 coffee
• Size H/8/5mm crochet hook or size needed to obtain gauge
• Tapestry needle

Tea Cozy
Gauge
13 hdc = 3¼ inches

Pattern Notes
Weave in ends as work progresses.

Join with slip stitch as indicated unless otherwise stated.

Chain-2 at beginning of rows counts as first double crochet unless otherwise stated.

Cozy
Row 1 (WS): With ranch red and leaving a 10-inch end for sewing, ch 33, hdc in 3rd ch from hook *(beg 2 sk chs count as a hdc)*, hdc in each rem ch across, turn. *(32 hdc)*

Row 2 (RS): Ch 2 *(see Pattern Notes)*, working in **back lps** *(see Stitch Guide)*, hdc in each hdc across, turn.

Rows 3–18: Rep row 2.

Row 19: Ch 2, working in back lps, hdc in each of next 10 hdc, ch 9 *(spout opening)*, sk next 9 hdc, hdc in each rem hdc, turn.

Row 20: Ch 2, working in back lps only, hdc in each hdc and in each ch across, turn.

Rows 21–38: Rep row 2. At end of last row, fasten off.

Tie

With ranch red, ch 50. Fasten off.

Stem

With coffee, ch 10, hdc in 3rd ch from hook, hdc in each rem ch across. Fasten off.

Small Leaf

Make 2.

With paddy green, ch 8, sc in 2nd ch from hook, hdc in each of next 2 chs, 2 dc in next ch, hdc in each of next 2 chs, 4 sc in last ch, working in unused lps on opposite side of starting ch, sc in each lp across, **join** (see Pattern Notes) in beg sc. Leaving an 8-inch end for sewing, fasten off. (17 sts)

Large Leaf

Make 2.

With paddy green, ch 10, sc in 2nd ch from hook, hdc in each of next 4 chs, 2 dc in next ch, hdc in each of next 3 chs, 4 sc in last ch, working in unused lps on opposite side of starting ch, hdc in each of next 3 lps, 2 dc in next lp, hdc in each of next 4 lps, join with a sl st in beg sc. Leaving an 8-inch end for sewing, fasten off. (23 sts)

Finishing

Step 1: With WS facing and with ranch red, sew first 6 sts of row 38 to first 6 sts in row 1. Sew last 9 sts of same rows tog, forming opening for handle.

Step 2: From WS, weave Tie through top of Cozy and use it to tighten and close top of Cozy.

Step 3: Sew Leaves and Stem to top of Cozy.

Step 4: Weave 20-inch strand of ranch red around bottom of Cozy and tie in bow after putting Cozy on teapot.

Coasters
Gauge
Rnds 1 & 2 = 2¼ inches

Pattern Notes
Weave in ends as work progresses.

Join with slip stitch as indicated unless otherwise stated.

Chain-3 at beginning of rounds counts as first double crochet unless otherwise stated.

Coaster
Make 2.

Rnd 1 (RS): With ranch red, ch 4, **join** (see Pattern Notes) in first ch to form a ring, **ch 3** (see Pattern Notes), 11 dc in ring, join in 3rd ch of beg ch-3. (12 dc)

Rnd 2: Ch 3, dc in same ch as joining, 2 dc in each rem dc around, join in 3rd ch of beg ch-3. (24 dc)

Rnd 3: Ch 3, dc in same ch as joining, dc in next dc, *2 dc in next dc, dc in next dc, rep from * around, join in 3rd ch of beg ch-3. (36 dc)

Rnd 4: Sl st in next dc, sc in next dc, 2 dc in each of next 3 dc, dc in next dc, 2 dc in next dc, hdc in next dc, sc in each of next 2 dc, sl st in each of next 3 dc, sc in next dc, dc in next dc, 2 dc in next dc, hdc in next dc, (sc, sl st) in next dc, sc in next dc, hdc in next dc, 2 dc in next dc, dc in next dc, sc in next dc, sl st in each of next 3 dc, sc in each of next 2 dc, hdc in next dc, 2 dc in next dc, dc in next dc, 2 dc in each of next 3 dc, sc in next dc, join in joining sl st. Fasten off.

Leaf
With paddy green, ch 6, sc in 2nd ch from hook, hdc in next ch, dc in next ch, hdc in next ch, (sc, sl st) in last ch. Fasten off. (6 sts)

Stem
With coffee, ch 5, sc in 2nd ch from hook, sc in each rem ch across. Fasten off. (4 sc)

Finishing
Sew Leaf and Stem to top center of Coaster. ●

Pineapple Bath Set
Continued from page 131

Row 2: Ch 3 *(see Pattern Notes)*, shell in ch-2 sp of next shell, ch 2, [shell in ch-2 sp of next shell] 3 times, ch 2, shell in ch-2 sp of next shell, dc in 3rd ch of beg 6 sk chs, turn.

Row 3: Ch 3, shell in ch-2 sp of next shell, ch 2, sc in ch-2 sp of next shell, 10 dc in ch-2 sp of next shell, sc in ch-2 sp of next shell, ch 2, shell in ch-2 sp of next shell, dc in 3rd ch of beg ch-3, turn. *(2 shells, 12 dc, 2 sc, 2 ch-2 sps)*

Row 4: Ch 3, shell in ch-2 sp of next shell, ch 2, sk next ch-2 sp, [dc in next dc, ch 1] 9 times, dc in next dc, ch 2, shell in ch-2 sp of next shell, dc in 3rd ch of beg ch-3, turn. *(2 shells, 12 dc, 2 ch-2 sps, 9 ch-1 sps)*

Row 5: Ch 3, shell in ch-2 sp of next shell, ch 2, sk next ch-2 sp, [sc in next ch-1 sp, ch 3] 8 times, sc in next ch-1 sp, ch 2, shell in ch-2 sp of next shell, dc in 3rd ch of beg ch-3, turn. *(2 shells, 2 dc, 9 sc, 8 ch-3 sps, 2 ch-2 sps)*

Row 6: Ch 3, shell in ch-2 sp of next shell, ch 2, sk next ch-2 sp, [sc in next ch-3 sp, ch 3] 7 times, sc in next ch-3 sp, ch 2, shell in ch-2 sp of next shell, dc in 3rd ch of beg ch-3, turn. *(2 shells, 2 dc, 8 sc, 7 ch-3 sps, 2 ch-2 sps)*

Row 7: Ch 3, shell in ch-2 sp of next shell, ch 2, sk next ch-2 sp, [sc in next ch-3 sp, ch 3] 6 times, sc in next ch-3 sp, ch 2, shell in ch-2

sp of next shell, dc in 3rd ch of beg ch-3, turn. *(2 shells, 2 dc, 7 sc, 6 ch-3 sps, 2 ch-2 sps)*

Row 8: Ch 3, shell in ch-2 sp of next shell, ch 2, sk next ch-2 sp, [sc in next ch-3 sp, ch 3] 5 times, sc in next ch-3 sp, ch 2, shell in ch-2 sp of next shell, dc in 3rd ch of beg ch-3, turn. *(2 shells, 2 dc, 6 sc, 5 ch-3 sps, 2 ch-2 sps)*

Row 9: Ch 3, shell in ch-2 sp of next shell, ch 2, sk next ch-2 sp, [sc in next ch-3 sp, ch 3] 4 times, sc in next ch-3 sp, ch 2, shell in ch-2 sp of next shell, dc in 3rd ch of beg ch-3, turn. *(2 shells, 2 dc, 5 sc, 4 ch-3 sps, 2 ch-2 sps)*

Row 10: Ch 3, (shell, ch 2, 2 dc) in ch-2 sp of next shell, ch 2, sk next ch-2 sp, [sc in next ch-3 sp, ch 3] 3 times, sc in next ch-3 sp, ch 2, (shell, ch 2, 2 dc) in ch-2 sp of next shell, dc in 3rd ch of beg ch-3, turn. *(2 shells, 6 dc, 4 sc, 3 ch-3 sps, 4 ch-2 sps)*

Row 11: Ch 3, shell in ch-2 sp of next shell, shell in next ch-2 sp, ch 2, sk next ch-2 sp, [sc in next ch-3 sp, ch 3] twice, sc in next ch-3 sp, ch 2, shell in ch-2 sp of next shell, shell in next ch-2 sp, dc in 3rd ch of beg ch-3, turn. *(4 shells, 2 dc, 3 sc, 2 ch-3 sps, 4 ch-2 sps)*

Row 12: Ch 3, [shell in ch-2 sp of next shell, ch 2] twice, sk next ch-2 sp, sc in next ch-3 sp, ch 3, sc in next ch-3 sp, [ch 2, shell in

145

ch-2 sp of next shell] twice, dc in 3rd ch of beg ch-3, turn. *(4 shells, 2 dc, 2 sc, 1 ch-3 sp, 4 ch-2 sps)*

Row 13: Ch 3, [shell in ch-2 sp of next shell, ch 2] twice, sk next ch-2 sp, sc in next ch-3 sp, [ch 2, shell in ch-2 sp of next shell] twice, dc in 3rd ch of beg ch-3, turn. *(4 shells, 2 dc, 1 sc, 4 ch-2 sps)*

Row 14: Ch 3, shell in ch-2 sp of next shell, ch 2, shell in ch-2 sp of next shell, tr in next sc, shell in ch-2 sp of next shell, ch 2, shell in ch-2 sp of next shell, dc in 3rd ch of beg ch-3, turn. *(4 shells, 2 dc, 1 tr, 2 ch-2 sps)*

Row 15: Ch 3, shell in ch-2 sp of next shell, [ch 2, shell in ch-2 sp of next shell] 3 times, dc in 3rd ch of beg ch-3. Fasten off. *(4 shells, 2 dc, 3 ch-2 sps)*

2nd Half

Row 1 (RS): Hold piece with RS facing and starting ch at top, **join** *(see Pattern Notes)* yarn in first ch, ch 3, shell in same ch as next shell on row 1 of First Half worked, ch 2, shell in same ch as each of next 3 shells on row 1 worked, ch 2, shell in same ch as next shell worked, sk next 2 chs of starting ch, dc in next ch, turn. *(5 shells, 2 dc, 2 ch-2 sps)*

Rows 2–15: Rep rows 2–15 of First Half. At end of row 15, **do not fasten off**.

Edging

Rnd 1 (RS): Working across next side, sl st in sp formed by last dc of row 15, ch 1, sc in same sp, *[ch 3, sc in sp formed by edge dc of next row] 29 times, [ch 3, sc in ch-2 sp of next shell, ch 3, sc in ch-2 sp between shells] 3 times, ch 3, sc in ch-3 sp of next shell, ch 3 **, working across next side, sc in sp formed by edge dc of shell, rep from * once, ending rep at **, join in beg sc. *(75 sc, 74 ch-3 sps)*

Rnd 2: Sl st in next ch-3 sp, ch 1, sc in same sp, ch 3, *sc in next ch-3 sp, ch 3, rep from * around, join in beg sc.

Rnd 3: Ch 1, 3 sc in each ch-3 sp around, join in beg sc. *(222 sc)*

Rnd 4: Ch 1, sc in each sc around, join in beg sc.

Rnds 5–7: Rep rnd 4.

Rnd 8: Ch 1, sc in each sc around, dec 18 sc evenly sp, join in beg sc. *(204 sc)*

Rnds 9 & 10: Rep rnd 8. *(168 sc at end of last rnd)*

Note: Tie ends of elastic tog to form ring. Size and tension of elastic will vary. Final adjustments can be done after placing on tank cover.

Rnd 11: Ch 1, hold elastic behind work, working over elastic, sc in each sc around, join in beg sc. Fasten off.

Finishing

Place piece over tank cover and adjust elastic if necessary. ●

146

Delicate Lace Table Runner

Continued from page 133

Row 8: Ch 3, shell in ch-2 sp of next shell, *ch 1, sk next ch-2 sp, sc in next dc, ch 1, shell in ch-2 sp of next shell, rep from * 3 times, ch 1, sc in 3rd ch of beg ch-3, turn. *(5 shells, 5 sc, 1 dc)*

Row 9: Ch 8, sl st in ch-2 sp of next shell, ch 8, sl st in 2nd dc of next shell, [ch 8, sl st in next sc, ch 8, sl st in ch-2 sp of next shell] 3 times, ch 8, sl st in 3rd ch of beg ch-3, turn. *(9 ch-8 sps)*

Row 10: Ch 6, sl st in first ch-8 sp, [ch 6, sl st in next sp] 8 times, turn. *(9 ch-6 sps)*

Row 11: Ch 3, 4 hdc in each ch-6 sp across, turn. *(37 sts)*

Border

Rnd 1: Ch 2, hdc in each of first 36 sts, 3 hdc in 3rd ch of beg ch-3, working across next side, 2 hdc in end of row 11, 4 hdc in next ch sp, hdc in last ch of same ch sp, hdc in end of next sc, hdc in same sp as sc worked, hdc in next ch sp, 4 hdc in sp formed by next edge dc, hdc in same sp as edge dc worked, hdc in next ch sp, 3 hdc in sp formed by next edge dc, 3 hdc in next ch sp, 2 hdc in end of next edge sc, 3 hdc in sp formed by edge dc of row 1, working across next side in unused lps of starting ch, hdc in each of next 36 chs, 3 hdc in last ch, working across next side, 3 hdc in next ch sp, hdc in each of next 2 chs of next ch sp, 2 hdc in sp formed by next edge dc, hdc in same dc, hdc in each of next 2 dc, 3 hdc in sp formed by next edge dc, 3 hdc in each of next 3 ch sps, 2 hdc in next ch sp, 5 hdc in sp formed by next edge hdc, join in beg hdc. *(134 hdc)*

Rnd 2: Ch 2, working in **back lps** *(see Stitch Guide)*, hdc in each hdc around, join in beg hdc. Fasten off.

Flower

Make 8.

Rnd 1 (RS): With medium dusty pink, ch 6, join in first ch to form a ring, *ch 15, sl st in ring, rep from * 4 times. *(5 ch-15 sps)*

Rnd 2: *Ch 18, sc in beg ring between next 2 sl sts, rep from * 4 times. Fasten off.

Assembly

Referring to diagram, sew Motifs together.

Edging

Join ecru in any hdc on rnd 2 of Border of any outer Motif, ch 1, sc in same hdc, sc in each rem hdc around, join in beg sc. Fasten off.

Finishing

Block lightly. Referring to photo for placement, sew Flowers to Table Runner. ●

Tweed Granny Rug

Continued from page 137

Remaining Motifs

Work 22 additional Motifs same as 2nd Motif, joining to adjacent Motifs in similar manner and making sure all 4-corner junctions are firmly joined. Join Motifs in 6 rows of 4 Motifs each.

Border

Rnd 1 (RS): Hold piece with RS facing and 1 short end at top, with 1 strand of falling leaves and 1 strand of claret held tog, join in center ch-2 sp to left of upper right-hand corner, ch 1, (sc, ch 2, sc) in same sp, *ch 2, sk next sc, next ch-2 sp and next sc, (sc, ch 2, sc) in next ch-2 sp, sk next sc, sc in next corner sp to right of joining, ch 2, sc in next corner sp to left of joining, sk next sc, (sc, ch 2, sc) in next ch-2 sp, ch 2, sk next sc, next ch-2 sp and next sc, (sc, ch 2, sc) in next ch-2 sp, rep from * twice, ch 2, sk next sc, next ch-2 sp and next sc, (sc, ch 2, sc) in next ch-2 sp, sk next sc, (sc, ch 4, sc) in next ch-4 sp (*corner*), sk next sc, (sc, ch 2, sc) in next ch-2 sp, ch 2, sk next sc, next ch-2 sp and next sc, (sc, ch 2, sc) in next ch-2 sp, **ch 2, sk next sc, next ch-2 sp and next sc, (sc, ch 2, sc) in next ch-2 sp, sk next sc, sc in next corner sp to right of joining, ch 2, sc in next corner sp to left of joining, sk next sc, (sc, ch 2, sc) in next ch-2 sp, ch 2, sk next sc, next ch-2 sp and next sc, (sc, ch

2, sc) in next ch-2 sp, rep from ** 4 times, ch 2, sk next sc, next ch-2 sp and next sc, (sc, ch 2, sc) in next ch-2 sp, sk next sc, (sc, ch 4, sc) in next ch-4 sp (*corner*), sk next sc, (sc, ch 2, sc) in next ch-2 sp, ch 2, sk next sc, next ch-2 sp and next sc, (sc, ch 2, sc) in next ch-2 sp, ***ch 2, sk next sc, next ch-2 sp and next sc, (sc, ch 2, sc) in next ch-2 sp, sk next sc, sc in next corner sp to right of joining, ch 2, sc in next corner sp to left of joining, sk next sc, (sc, ch 2, sc) in next ch-2 sp, ch 2, sk next sc, next ch-2 sp and next sc, (sc, ch 2, sc) in next ch-2 sp, rep from *** twice, ch 2, sk next sc, next ch-2 sp and next sc, (sc, ch 2, sc) in next ch-2 sp, sk next sc, (sc, ch 4, sc) in next ch-4 sp (*corner*), sk next sc, (sc, ch 2, sc) in next ch-2 sp, ch 2, sk next sc, next ch-2 sp and next sc, (sc, ch 2, sc) in next ch-2 sp, ****ch 2, sk next sc, next ch-2 sp and next sc, (sc, ch 2, sc) in next ch-2 sp, sk next sc, sc in next corner sp to right of joining, ch 2, sc in next corner sp to left of joining, sk next sc, (sc, ch 2, sc) in next ch-2 sp, ch 2, sk next sc, next ch-2 sp and next sc, (sc, ch 2, sc) in next ch-2 sp, rep from **** 4 times, ch 2, sk next sc, next ch-2 sp and next sc, (sc, ch 2, sc) in next ch-2 sp, sk next sc, (sc, ch 4, sc) in next ch-4 sp *(corner)*, sk next sc, (sc, ch 2, sc) in next ch-2 sp, ch 2, join in beg sc. Fasten off.

Note: Divide rem claret in half and use 2 strands held tog as 1 on following rnd.

Rnd 2: Hold piece with RS facing and 1 short end at top, with 2 strands of claret held tog as 1, join in 2nd ch-2 sp to left of upper right-hand corner, ch 1, (sc, ch 2, sc) in same sp, *sc in next ch-2 sp, (sc, ch 2, sc) in each of next 3 ch-2 sps, sc in next ch-2 sp, (sc, ch 2, sc) in next ch-2 sp, rep from * twice, sc in next ch-2 sp, (sc, ch 2, sc) in next ch-2 sp, ch 1, (sc, ch 2, sc, ch 3, ch 2, sc) in next corner ch-4 sp *(corner)*, ch 1, (sc, ch 2, sc) in next ch-2 sp, sc in next ch-2 sp, (sc, ch 2, sc) in next ch-2 sp, **sc in next ch-2 sp, (sc, ch 2, sc) in each of next 3 ch-2 sps, sc in next ch-2 sp, (sc, ch 2, sc) in next ch-2 sp, rep from ** 4 times, sc in next ch-2 sp, (sc, ch 2, sc) in next ch-2 sp, ch 1, (sc, ch 2, sc, ch 3, sc, ch 2, sc) in next corner ch-4 sp *(corner)*, ch 1, (sc, ch 2, sc) in next ch-2 sp, sc in next sc, (sc, ch 2, sc) in next ch-2 sp, ***sc in next ch-2 sp, (sc, ch 2, sc) in each of next 3 ch-2 sps, sc in next ch-2 sp, (sc, ch 2, sc) in next ch-2 sp, rep from *** twice, sc in next ch-2 sp, (sc, ch 2, sc) in next ch-2 sp, ch 1, (sc, ch 2, sc, ch 3, sc, ch 2, sc) in next corner ch-4 sp *(corner)*, ch 1, (sc, ch 2, sc) in next ch-2 sp, sc in next sc, (sc, ch 2, sc) in next ch-2 sp, ****sc in next ch-2 sp, (sc, ch 2, sc) in each of next 3 ch-2 sps, sc in next ch-2 sp, (sc, ch 2, sc) in next ch-2 sp, rep from **** 4 times, sc in next ch-2 sp, (sc, ch 2, sc) in next ch-2 sp, ch 1, (sc, ch 2, sc, ch 3, sc, ch 2, sc) in next corner ch-4 sp *(corner)*, ch 1, (sc, ch 2, sc) in next ch-2 sp, sc in next ch-2 sp, join in beg sc. Fasten off. ●

Just Throws & Pillows

Make a simple throw and matching pillow, each one using only three skeins of yarn. These hand-stitched projects are great for quick and easy gifts.

Mum Lapghan & Pillow

Designs by *Rena V. Stevens*

Skill Level

EASY

Finished Size
Lapghan: 31 inches x 45½ inches
Pillow: 16 inches x 16 inches

Materials
Lapghan
• TLC Essentials medium (worsted) weight yarn (6 oz/312 yds/170g per skein):
  1 skein each #2254 persimmon, #2919 barn red, #2936 claret
• Size K/10½/6.5mm crochet hook or size needed to obtain gauge
• Tapestry needle
Pillow
• TLC Essentials medium (worsted) weight yarn (6 oz/312 yds/170g per skein):
  1 skein each #2254 persimmon, #2919 barn red, #2936 claret
• Sizes I/9/5.5mm and J/10/6mm crochet hooks or size needed to obtain gauge
• Tapestry needle

Lapghan
Gauge
11 dc = 4 inches

Pattern Notes
Weave in ends as work progresses.

Join with slip stitch as indicated unless otherwise stated.

Chain-3 at beginning of rows counts as first double crochet unless otherwise stated.

Lapghan
Row 1 (WS): With persimmon, ch 85 loosely, dc in 5th ch from hook *(beg 4 sk chs count as a dc)*, dc in each rem ch across, turn. *(82 dc)*

Row 2 (RS): Ch 6, drop lp from hook, **join** *(see Pattern Notes)* barn red in **front lp** *(see Stitch Guide)* of first dc, **ch 3** *(see Pattern Notes)*, working in front lps, dc in each rem dc across, turn.

Row 3: Ch 6, drop lp from hook, join claret in front lp of first dc, ch 3, working in front lps, dc in each rem dc across, turn.

Row 4: Ch 6, drop lp from hook, with ch-6 in front of work, insert hook in lp dropped 3 rows below, working in front lps, sl st in first dc, ch 3, dc in each rem dc across, turn.

Rep row 4 until piece measures approximately 45 inches, ending with a claret row. At end of last row, fasten off.

Last row: Insert hook in persimmon lp dropped 3 rows below, working in front lps only, sl st in first dc, ch 3, dc in each rem dc across. Fasten off.

Insert hook in barn red lp dropped 2 rows below, sl st through both lps of 3rd ch of beg ch-3 of last row. Fasten off.

Reduce number of chs in rem claret lp dropped 2 rows below to 3 chs, sl st through both lps of 3rd ch of beg ch-3 of last row. Fasten off.

If desired, work edge chs at sides of beg rows to match rest of side edge.

Edging

Hold piece with RS facing and last row at top, join claret in sp between last 2 dc of last row at left-hand corner, ch 2, working left to right, work [**reverse sc** *(see Fig. 1)*, ch 1] twice in same sp, working in sps between dc, *sk next sp, reverse sc in next sp, ch 1, rep from * across to last sp, [reverse sc, ch 1] twice in last sp, sl st in same sp. Fasten off.

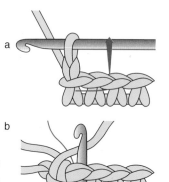

a

b

c

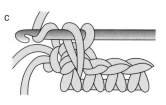

Fig. 1
Reverse Single Crochet

Hold piece with RS facing and starting ch at top, join claret in sp between last 2 dc of first row at left-hand corner, ch 2, working left to right, work (reverse sc, ch 1) twice in same sp, working in sps between dc, *sk next sp, reverse sc in next sp, ch 1, rep from * across to last sp, [reverse sc, ch 1] twice in last sp, sl st in same sp. Fasten off.

Pillow
Gauge
Size J hook: 12 hdc = 4 inches

Pattern Notes
Weave in ends as work progresses.

Join with slip stitch as indicated unless otherwise stated.

Chain-2 at beginning of rows counts as first half double crochet unless otherwise stated.

Special Stitch
Picot: Ch 3, sl st in **front lp** *(see Stitch Guide)* of 3rd ch from hook.

Pillow
Front
Panel A
Row 1 (WS): With size J hook and persimmon, ch 34 loosely, hdc in 4th ch from hook *(beg 4 sk chs count as a hdc)*, hdc in each rem ch across. Fasten off. Turn. *(32 hdc)*

Row 2 (RS): Join *(see Pattern Notes)* barn red in first hdc, **ch 2** *(see Pattern Notes)*, hdc in each hdc across. Fasten off. Turn.

Row 3: Join claret in first hdc, ch 2, hdc in each hdc across. Fasten off.

Row 4: Join persimmon in first hdc, ch 2, hdc in each hdc across. Fasten off.

Rows 5–25: [Rep rows 2–4 consecutively] 7 times.

Rows 26 & 27: Rep rows 2 and 3.

Panel B

Row 1 (WS): With size J hook and persimmon, ch 16 loosely, hdc in 4th ch from hook (*beg 4 sk chs count as a hdc*), hdc in each rem ch across, turn. (*14 hdc*)

Row 2 (RS): Ch 2, hdc in each hdc across to beg 4 sk chs, hdc in 4th ch of beg 4 sk chs, turn.

Rows 3–27: Rep row 2. At end of last row, fasten off.

Panel C

Row 1 (WS): With size J hook and persimmon, ch 48 loosely, hdc in 4th ch from hook (*beg 4 sk chs count as a hdc*), hdc in each rem ch across, turn. (*46 hdc*)

Row 2 (RS): Ch 2, hdc in each hdc across to beg 4 sk chs, hdc in 4th ch of beg 4 sk chs, turn.

Rows 3–8: Rep row 2. At end of last row, fasten off.

Flower

Make 1 of each color.

Rnd 1 (RS): With size I hook, ch 4, join in first ch to form a ring, [sl st in ring, **picot** (*see Special Stitch*)] 4 times, join in beg sl st.

Rnd 2: [Ch 1, working behind picots, sl st in **back lp** (*see Stitch Guide*) of next sl st] 4 times.

Rnd 3: [(Sc, dc, 3 tr, dc) in next ch-1 sp] 4 times (*4 petals*), join in back lp of beg sc. (*4 petals*)

Note: *On following round, work sl sts by inserting hook from WS between sts into ch-1 sps of rnd 2.*

Rnd 4: Ch 1, sl st in sp before sc of same petal, ch 3, sl st between first and 2nd tr of same petal, ch 3, *sl st in sp before sc of next petal, ch 3, sl st between first and 2nd tr of same petal, ch 3, rep from * around, join in beg sl st. (*8 ch-3 sps*)

Rnd 5: (Sc, dc, 3 tr, dc, sc) in each ch-3 sp (*8 petals*), join in back lp of beg sc. (*8 petals*)

Back

Row 1 (WS): With size J hook and barn red, ch 48 loosely, hdc in 4th ch from hook (*beg 4 sk chs count as a hdc*), hdc in each rem ch across, turn. (*46 hdc*)

Row 2 (RS): Ch 2, hdc in each hdc across to beg 4 sk chs, hdc in 4th ch of beg 4 sk chs, turn.

Rows 3–35: Rep row 2. At end of last row, fasten off.

Assembly

Referring to diagram for placement, join Panels A, B, and C for Front piece. Hold Panels A and B with WS tog, starting chs to right, and Panel A facing, working through both thicknesses and with size J hook, join claret in end of first row at left-hand edge, ch 2, working left to right, work **reverse sc** (*see Fig. 1, page 154*) in same sp, *ch 1, reverse sc in end of next row, rep from * across, sl st in same row as last reverse sc made. Fasten off.

Continued on page 171

Roaming Cables Lapghan & Pillow

Designs by *Darla Sims*

Finished Size
Lapghan: 45½ inches x 67 inches
Pillow: 18 inches x 18 inches

Materials
Lapghan
• Caron One Pound medium (worsted) weight yarn (16 oz/812 yds/454g per skein):
   3 skeins #562 claret
• Sizes K/10½/6.5mm and L/11/8mm crochet hooks or size needed to obtain gauge
• Tapestry needle
Pillow
• Caron One Pound medium (worsted) weight yarn (16 oz/812 yds/454g per skein):
   1 skein #562 claret
• Sizes K/10½/6.5mm and L/11/8mm crochet hooks or size needed to obtain gauge
• Tapestry needle
• 18-inch x 18-inch pillow form

Lapghan
Gauge
Size L hook: 8 sts = 4 inches

Pattern Notes
Weave in ends as work progresses.

Chain-2 at beginning of rows counts as first double crochet unless otherwise stated.

Chain-3 at beginning of rows counts as first double crochet unless otherwise stated.

Special Stitches
Popcorn (pc): 4 sc in indicated st, remove hook, insert hook from back to front through first and 4th sc, yo, draw lp through sc.

Shell: 3 dc in indicated st.

Afghan
Center Panel
Row 1 (RS): With size L hook, ch 41, working in back bar of chs, hdc in 3rd ch from hook (*beg 2 sk chs count as a hdc*), hdc in each rem ch across, turn. (*40 hdc*)

Row 2: Ch 2 (*see Pattern Notes*), hdc in each hdc across, hdc in 2nd ch of beg 2 sk chs, turn.

156

Row 3: Ch 2, hdc in next hdc, *sk next 2 hdc on 2nd row below, **fpdc** (*see Stitch Guide*) around each of next 2 hdc on 2nd row below, working in front of fpdc just made, fpdc around each sk hdc on 2nd row **, on working row, sk hdc behind fpdc, hdc in each of next 4 hdc, rep from * 4 times, ending last rep at **, hdc in last hdc, hdc in 2nd ch of beg ch-2, turn.

Row 4: Ch 2, hdc in each hdc across, hdc in 2nd ch of beg ch-2, turn.

Note: *On following rows, always sk sts on working row behind fpdc.*

Row 5: Ch 2, hdc in next hdc, *sk next 2 fpdc, fpdc around each of next 2 fpdc, working in front of fpdc just made, fpdc around each sk fpdc **, hdc in each of next 4 hdc, rep from * 4 times, ending last rep at **, hdc in last hdc, hdc in 2nd ch of beg ch-2, turn.

Row 6: Rep row 4.

Row 7: Ch 2, *fpdc around each of next 2 fpdc, hdc in each of next 2 hdc, fpdc around each of next 2 fpdc**, rep from * 4 times, ending last rep at **, hdc in 2nd ch of beg ch-2, turn.

Row 8: Rep row 4.

Row 9: Ch 2, *fpdc around each of next 2 fpdc, hdc in each of next 2 hdc, fpdc around each of next 2 fpdc **, rep from * 4 times, ending last rep at **, hdc in 2nd ch of beg ch-2, turn.

Row 10: Rep row 4.

Row 11: Ch 2, hdc in next hdc, *fpdc around each of next 4 fpdc, hdc in each of next 4 hdc, rep from * 3 times, fpdc around each of next 4 fpdc, hdc in last hdc, hdc in 2nd ch of beg ch-2, turn.

Row 12: Rep row 4.

Row 13: Ch 2, hdc in next hdc, *sk next 2 fpdc, fpdc around each of next 2 fpdc, working in front of 2 fpdc just made, fpdc around each sk fpdc **, hdc in each of next 4 hdc, rep from * 4 times, ending last rep at **, hdc in last hdc, hdc in 2nd ch of beg ch-2, turn.

Row 14: Rep row 4.

Row 15: Ch 2, hdc in next hdc, *sk next 2 fpdc, fpdc around each of next 2 fpdc, working in front of 2 fpdc just made, fpdc around each sk fpdc **, hdc in each of next 4 hdc, rep from * 4 times, ending last rep at **, hdc in last hdc, hdc in 2nd ch of beg ch-2, turn.

Rows 16–103: [Rep rows 8–15 consecutively] 11 times. At end of last row, fasten off.

Right Side Panel

Row 1 (RS): Hold piece with RS facing and starting ch to right, with size K hook, join yarn with sc in end of row 1, working in ends of rows, work 143 sc evenly sp across, turn. (*144 sc*)

Row 2: Ch 1, **fpsc** *(see Stitch Guide)* around each sc across, turn.

Row 3: Ch 3 *(see Pattern Notes)*, dc in each sc across, turn.

Row 4: Ch 1, sc in each of first 2 dc, *pc *(see Special Stitches)* in next dc, sc in each of next 3 dc, rep from * 34 times, pc in next dc, sc in 3rd ch of beg ch-3, turn. *(36 pc, 108 sc)*

Row 5: Ch 3, dc in each st across, turn. *(144 dc)*

Row 6: Ch 1, fpsc around each dc across, turn.

Row 7: With size K hook, ch 3, *sk next 2 sts, **shell** *(see Special Stitches)* in next st, rep from * 46 times, sk next 2 sts, dc in last st, turn. *(47 shells, 2 dc)*

Row 8: Ch 3, dc in sp between first dc and next dc, shell in each sp between shells across to sp between last shell and beg ch-3, dc in sp between last shell and beg ch-3, dc in 3rd ch of beg ch-3, turn. *(46 shells, 4 dc)*

Row 9: Ch 3, shell in sp between shells across to sp between last shell and next dc, shell in sp between last shell and next dc, dc in 3rd ch of beg ch-3.

Rows 10–17: [Rep rows 8 and 9 alternately] 4 times.

Row 18: Rep row 8. At end of row, fasten off.

Left Side Panel

Row 1 (RS): Hold piece with RS facing and row 103 to right, with size K hook, join yarn with sc in end of row 103, working in ends of rows, work 143 sc evenly spaced across, turn. *(144 sc)*

Rows 2–18: Rep rows 2–18 of Right Side Panel.

Border

Rnd 1 (RS): Hold piece with RS facing and starting ch of Center Panel at top, with size K hook, join yarn with sc in right-hand corner, sc in same sp *(beg corner)*, working across bottom, work 102 sc evenly sp to next corner, 3 sc in corner *(corner)*, working across next side, work 141 sc to next corner, 3 sc in corner *(corner)*, working across next side, work 102 sc evenly sp to next corner, 3 sc in corner *(corner)*, working across next side, work 141 sc evenly sp across to beg sc, sc in same sp as beg 2 sc, join to beg sc, turn. *(498 sc)*

Rnd 2: Ch 1, fpsc around each sc around, join in first st, turn.

Rnd 3: Ch 3, dc in each of next 104 sts, 3 dc in next st *(corner)*, dc in each of next 143 sts, 3 dc in next st *(corner)*, dc in each of next 104 sts, 3 dc in next st *(corner)*, dc in each of next 143 sts, 2 dc in same st as beg ch-3 *(corner)*, join in 3rd ch of beg ch-3, turn. *(506 dc)*

Continued on page 171

Man's Diamond Lapghan & Pillow

Designs by *Rena V. Stevens*

Skill Level

EASY

Finished Size
Lapghan: 35 inches x 43½ inches
Pillow: 17 inches x 17 inches

Materials
Lapghan
• Red Heart Fiesta medium (worsted) weight yarn (6 oz/316 yds/170g per skein):
  2 skeins #6341 millennium
• TLC Heathers medium (worsted) weight yarn (5 oz/260 yds/141g per skein):
  1 skein #2480 charcoal
• Size J/10/6mm crochet hook or size needed to obtain gauge
• Tapestry needle
• Stitch markers

Pillow
• Red Heart Fiesta medium (worsted) weight yarn (6 oz/316 yds/170g per skein):
  1 skein #6341 millennium
• TLC Heathers medium (worsted) weight yarn (5 oz/260 yds/141g per skein):
  1 skein #2480 charcoal
• Size J/10/6mm crochet hook or size needed to obtain gauge
• Tapestry needle
• 16-inch x 16-inch pillow form
• Stitch markers

Lapghan
Gauge
14 hdc = 4 inches

Pattern Notes
Weave in ends as work progresses.

Join with slip stitch as indicated unless otherwise stated.

Chain-3 at beginning of rows counts as first half double crochet unless otherwise stated.

Chain-6 at beginning of rows counts as first double crochet and chain-3 space unless otherwise stated.

Lapghan
Motif
Make 18.

Row 1 (RS): With millennium, ch 4, hdc in 4th ch from hook, turn.

Note: *Remainder of piece is worked in* **back lps** *(see Stitch Guide).*

Row 2: Ch 3 *(see Pattern Notes)*, hdc in first hdc, hdc in next ch, 2 hdc in next ch, turn. *(5 sts)*

Row 3: Ch 3, hdc in first hdc, hdc in each hdc across to last hdc, 2 hdc in last hdc, turn. *(7 sts)*

Rows 4–12: Rep row 3. *(25 sts at end of last row)*

Note: *Mark both ends of row 12 as midpoint of motif.*

Row 13: Ch 3, **hdc dec** (*see Stitch Guide*) in next 2 hdc, hdc in each hdc across to last 2 hdc, sk next hdc, hdc in last hdc, turn. (*23 sts*)

Rows 14–22: Rep row 13. (*5 sts at end of last row*)

Row 23: Ch 3, hdc dec in next 2 hdc, sk next hdc, hdc in last hdc, turn. (*3 sts*)

Row 24: Ch 1, sk first 2 hdc, hdc in last hdc. Fasten off.

Edging

Hold Motif with RS facing, **join** *(see Pattern Notes)* charcoal in the end of row 13, **ch 6** *(see Pattern Notes)*, *[dc in next row, ch 1] 11 times, dc in 1 lp at edge of point, ch 1, (tr, ch 2, dtr, ch 2, tr) in point, ch 1, dc in 1 lp at opposite edge of same point, ch 1, [dc in next row, ch 1] 10 times **, dc in next row, ch 3, [dc in next row, ch 1] 11 times, rep from * once, ending rep at **, join in 3rd ch of beg ch-6. Fasten off.

Assembly

Referring to diagram for placement, join Motifs in diagonal strips. To join Motifs, hold 2 Motifs with WS tog, matching top point of front Motif to marked ch-3 sp of back Motif, working through both thicknesses at same time in ends of matching rows, with millennium, make slip knot on hook, sc in dtr at point of front Motif and ch-3 sp of back Motif, sc in same sp, ch 1, sc in next ch-2 sp on front Motif and in same ch-3 sp on back Motif, ch 1, sc in same ch-2 sp on front Motif and in next ch-1 sp on back Motif, ch 1, [sc in next ch-1 sp on both Motifs, ch 1] 11 times, sc in next ch-1 sp on front Motif and in next ch-2 sp on back Motif, ch 1, sc in next ch-3 sp of front Motif and in same ch-2 sp of back Motif, ch 1, 3 sc in same ch-3 sp of front Motif and in next dtr of back Motif. Fasten off.

Join strips in same manner, working 1 sc instead of 2 sc in joining sts wherever they occupy corresponding sts at joinings.

Pillow

Gauge

11 dc = 4 inches

Pattern Notes

Weave in ends as work progresses.

Join with slip stitch as indicated unless otherwise stated.

Chain-3 at beginning of rows counts as first half double crochet unless otherwise stated.

Special Stitches

Picot: Ch 2, sl st in **front lp** *(see Stitch Guide)* of 2nd ch from hook.

Large picot (lg picot): Ch 3, sl st in front lp of 3rd ch from hook.

Pillow

Front

Row 1 (RS): With millennium, ch 42 loosely, dc in 4th ch from hook *(beg 3 sk chs count as a dc)*, dc in each rem ch across, turn. *(40 dc)*

Row 2: Ch 3 *(see Pattern Notes)*, dc in each dc across, turn.

Rows 3–26: Rep row 2. At end of last row, fasten off.

Motif

Make 4.

Row 1 (RS): With millennium, ch 4, hdc in 4th ch from hook, turn.

Note: *Remainder of piece is worked in* **back lps** *(see Stitch Guide).*

Row 2: Ch 3 (see *Pattern Notes*), hdc in first hdc, hdc in next ch, 2 hdc in next ch, turn. (5 sts)

Row 3: Ch 3, hdc in first hdc, hdc in each hdc across to last hdc, 2 hdc in last hdc, turn. (7 sts)

Rows 4–6: Rep row 3. (13 sts at end of last row)

Note: Mark both ends of row 6 as midpoint of Motif.

Row 7: Ch 3, hdc dec (see *Stitch Guide*) in next 2 hdc, hdc in each hdc across to last 2 hdc, sk next hdc, hdc in last hdc, turn. (11 sts)

Rows 8–10: Rep row 7. (5 sts at end of last row)

Row 11: Ch 3, hdc dec in next 2 hdc, sk next hdc, hdc in last hdc, turn. (3 sts)

Row 12: Ch 1, sk first 2 hdc, hdc in last hdc. Fasten off.

Assembly

Referring to diagram for placement, join Motifs in 2 diagonal strips. To join Motifs, hold 2 Motifs with WS tog, matching top point of front Motif to marked row of back Motif, working through both thickness at same time in ends of matching rows, join (see *Pattern Notes*) millennium in point of front Motif and in row 6 of back Motif, ch 1, sc in same sp, *ch 1, sc in next row, rep from * across to row 6 of front Motif, ch 1, 2 sc in row 6. Fasten off. Join rem Motifs in same manner.

Edging

Hold piece with RS and point of bottom Motif at top, join charcoal in end of row 1, ch 1, sc in same sp, picot (see *Special Stitches*), working in ends of rows of Motifs, [sc in next row, picot] 22 times, (sc, lg picot—see *Special Stitches*, sc) in end of point, [sc in next row, picot] 23 times, (sc, lg picot, sc) in end of point, join in beg sc. Fasten off.

Back

With charcoal, work same as Front.

Pillow Assembly

Referring to photo for placement, place joined Motifs on Front. Holding millennium beneath work, sl st loosely alternately around edges of Motifs, working in same sps as Edging sts.

Hold Front and Back with WS tog and Front facing, working through both thicknesses at same time, join charcoal with sc in end of first row in bottom right-hand corner, picot, sc in same sp, picot, working across side in ends of rows, *sc in next row, picot, rep from * across to last row, (sc, lg picot) twice in last row, working across next side in sps between sts, **sk next 2 dc, sc in next sp, picot, rep from ** across to 2nd sp from next corner, sk next 2 dc, (sc, lg picot) twice in last sp, working across side in ends of rows, ***sc in next row, picot, rep from *** across to last row, (sc, lg picot) twice in last row, working across next side in sps between sts, ****sk next 2 dc, sc in next sp, picot, rep from **** across to beg sc, join in beg sc. Fasten off. ●

Rainbow Lapghan & Pillow

Designs by *Glenda Winkleman*

Finished Size
Lapghan: 42 inches x 52½ inches
Pillow: 16 inches x 16 inches, including edging

Materials
Lapghan
- Red Heart Super Saver Jumbo medium (worsted) weight yarn (16 oz/ 835 yds/438g per skein):
  2 skeins #316 soft white
- Red Heart Super Saver Economy medium (worsted) weight yarn (5 oz/244 yds/141g per skein):
  1 skein #723 piñata print
- TLC Essentials medium (worsted) weight yarn (6 oz/ 312 yds/170g per skein):
  1 oz/ 50 yds/28g #2680 Eden green
- Size J/10/6mm crochet hook or size needed to obtain gauge
- Tapestry needle

Lapghan
Gauge
Rnds 1–5 = 5½ inches

Pattern Notes
Weave in ends as work progresses.

Join with slip stitch as indicated unless otherwise stated.

Chain-3 at beginning of rounds counts as first double crochet unless otherwise stated.

Special Stitches
Beginning popcorn (beg pc): Ch 3, 2 dc in ring, remove hook, insert hook in 3rd ch of beg ch-3, draw dropped lp through lp on hook.

Popcorn (pc): 3 dc in ring, remove hook, insert hook in first dc, draw dropped lp through st on hook.

Long treble crochet (lng tr): Yo twice, insert hook in indicated sp, yo, draw lp up to height of working row, [yo, draw through 2 lps on hook] 3 times.

Lapghan
Square
Make 20.

Rnd 1 (RS): With piñata print, ch 5, **join** (*see Pattern Notes*) in first ch to form a ring, **beg pc** (*see Special Stitches*) in ring, ch 3, [pc *(see Special Stitches)* in ring, ch 3] 7 times, join in top of beg pc. Fasten off. *(8 pc, 8 ch-3 sps)*

Rnd 2: Join Eden green in first ch-3 sp, **ch 3** *(see Pattern Notes)*, (2 dc, ch 2, 3 dc) in same sp *(beg corner)*, ch 2, sk next ch-3 sp, *(3 dc, ch 2, 3 dc) in next ch-3 sp *(corner)*, ch 2, sk next ch-3 sp, rep from * twice, join in 3rd ch of beg ch-3. Fasten off. *(24 dc, 8 ch-2 sps)*

Rnd 3: Join soft white in any corner ch-2 sp, ch 3, (2 dc, ch 2, 3 dc) in same sp *(beg corner)*, sk next 3 dc, 3 **lng tr** *(see Special Stitches)* in next ch-2 sp on 2nd rnd below, sk next 3 dc, *(3 dc, ch 2, 3 dc) in same sp *(corner)*, sk next 3 dc, 3 lng tr in next ch-2 sp on 2nd rnd below, sk next 3 dc , rep from * twice, join in 3rd ch of beg ch-3. *(12 lng tr, 24 dc, 4 ch-2 sps)*

Rnd 4: Sl st in each of next 2 dc, sl st in next ch-2 sp, ch 3, (2 dc, ch 2, 3 dc) in same sp *(beg corner)*, sk next dc, [2 dc in next dc, sk next dc] 4 times, *(3 dc, ch 2, 3 dc) in next corner ch-2 sp *(corner)*, sk next dc, [2 dc in next dc, sk next dc] 4 times, rep from * around, join in 3rd ch of beg ch-3. Fasten off. *(56 dc)*

Rnd 5: Join piñata print in any corner ch-2 sp, ch 1, (sc, ch 2, sc) in same sp *(corner)*, [ch 1, sk next dc, sc in next dc] 7 times, *(sc, ch 2, sc) in next corner ch-2 sp *(corner)*, [ch 1, sk next dc, sc in next dc] 7 times, ch 1, rep from * around, join in beg sc. Fasten off. *(36 sc, 4 ch-2 sps, 32 ch-1 sps)*

Rnd 6: Join soft white in any corner ch-2 sp, ch 3, (dc, ch 2, 2 dc) in same sp *(beg corner)*, dc in each sc and each ch-1 sp across to next corner ch-2 sp, *(2 dc, ch 2, 2 dc) in corner ch-2 sp *(corner)*, dc in each sc and each ch-1 sp across to next corner ch-2 sp, rep from * around, join in 3rd ch of beg ch-3. *(84 dc, 4 ch-2 sps)*

Rnd 7: Ch 3, dc in each dc around, working (2 dc, ch 2, 2 dc) in each corner ch-2 sp, join in 3rd ch of beg ch-3. *(100 dc, 4 ch-2 sps)*

Rnd 8: Ch 1, sc in same ch as joining, sc in each dc around, working (sc, ch 2, sc) in each corner ch-2 sp, join in beg sc. *(104 sc, 4 ch-2 sps)*

Rnd 9: Ch 3, dc in each sc around, working (2 dc, ch 2, 2 dc) in each corner ch-2 sp, join in 3rd ch of beg ch-3. *(124 dc, 4 ch-2 sps)*

Rnd 10: Rep rnd 7. At end of rnd, fasten off. *(140 dc, 4 ch-2 sps)*

Assembly

Join Squares in 5 rows of 4 Squares each. To join Squares, hold 2 Squares with RS tog, working through both thicknesses, join soft white in ch-2 sp of right-hand corner, ch 1, sc in same sp, working in **back lps** *(see Stitch Guide)* only, sc in each dc across to next corner ch-2 sp, sc in corner ch-2 sp. Fasten off. Join rem Squares in same manner.

Border

Rnd 1 (RS): Hold piece with RS facing and 1 short end at top, join soft white in ch-2 sp in upper right-hand corner, ch 1, 3 sc in same ch-2 sp *(corner)*, working around outer edge, sc in each dc and in each ch sp on each side of each joining and work 3 sc in each corner ch-2 sp, join in beg sc. Fasten off.

Rnd 2: Join Eden green in same sc as joining, ch 1, hdc in each sc around, join in beg hdc. Fasten off.

Pillow

Gauge

Rnds 1–5 = 5½ inches

Pattern Notes

Weave in ends as work progresses.

Join with slip stitch as indicated unless otherwise stated.

Chain-3 at beginning of rounds counts as first double crochet unless otherwise stated.

Special Stitches

Beginning popcorn (beg pc): Ch 3, 2 dc in ring, remove hook, insert hook in 3rd ch of beg ch-3, draw dropped lp through lp on hook.

Popcorn (pc): 3 dc in ring, remove hook, insert hook in first dc, draw dropped lp through st on hook.

Long treble crochet (lng tr): Yo twice, insert hook in indicated sp, yo, draw lp up to height of working row, [yo, draw through 2 lps on hook] 3 times.

Pillow

Motif

Make 20.

Rnd 1 (RS): With piñata print, ch 5, **join** (*see Pattern Notes*) in first ch to form a ring, **beg pc** (*see Special Stitches*) in ring, ch 3, [**pc** (*see Special Stitches*) in ring, ch 3] 7 times, join in top of beg pc. Fasten off. (*8 pc, 8 ch-3 sps*)

Rnd 2: Join Eden green in first ch-3 sp, **ch 3** (*see Pattern Notes*), (2 dc, ch 2, 3 dc) in same sp (*beg corner*), ch 2, sk next ch-3 sp, *(3 dc, ch 2, 3 dc) in next ch-3 sp (*corner*), ch 2, sk next ch-3 sp, rep from * twice, join in 3rd ch of beg ch-3. Fasten off. (*24 dc, 8 ch-2 sps*)

Rnd 3: Join soft white in any corner ch-2 sp, ch 3, (2 dc, ch 2, 3 dc) in same sp (*beg corner*), sk next 3 dc, 3 **lng tr** (*see Special Stitches*) in next ch-2 sp on 2nd rnd below, sk next 3 dc, *(3 dc, ch 2, 3 dc) in same sp (*corner*), sk next 3 dc, 3 lng tr in next ch-2 sp on 2nd rnd below, sk next 3 dc, rep from * twice, join in 3rd ch of beg ch-3. (*12 lng tr, 24 dc, 4 ch-2 sps*)

Rnd 4: Sl st in each of next 2 dc, sl st in next ch-2 sp, ch 3, (2 dc, ch 2, 3 dc) in same sp (*beg corner*), sk next dc, [2 dc in next dc, sk next dc] 4 times, *(3 dc, ch 2, 3 dc) in next corner ch-2 sp (*corner*), sk next dc, [2 dc in next dc, sk next dc] 4 times, rep from * around, join in 3rd ch of beg ch-3. Fasten off. (*56 dc*)

Rnd 5: Join piñata print in any corner ch-2 sp, ch 1, (sc, ch 2, sc) in same sp (*corner*), [ch 1, sk next dc, sc in next dc] 7 times, *(sc, ch 2, sc) in next corner ch-2 sp (*corner*), [ch 1, sk next dc, sc in next dc] 7 times, ch 1, rep from * around, join in beg sc. Fasten off. (*36 sc, 4 ch-2 sps, 32 ch-1 sps*)

Rnd 6: Join soft white in any corner ch-2 sp, ch 3, (dc, ch 2, 2 dc) in same sp (*beg corner*), dc in each sc and each ch-1 sp across to next corner ch-2 sp, *(2 dc, ch 2, 2 dc) in corner ch-2 sp (*corner*), dc in each sc and each ch-1 sp across to next corner ch-2 sp, rep from * around, join in 3rd ch of beg ch-3. Fasten off. (*84 dc, 4 ch-2 sps*)

Continued on page 174

Materials

Pillow

- Red Heart Super Saver medium (worsted) weight yarn (solids: 7 oz/364 yds/198g; prints: 5 oz/244 yds/141g per skein):
  - 1 skein #316 soft white
    2 oz/100 yds/56g #723 piñata print
- TLC Essentials medium (worsted) weight yarn (6 oz/312 yds/170g per skein):
  - 1 skein #2680 Eden green
- Size J/10/6mm crochet hook or size needed to obtain gauge
- Tapestry needle
- 14-inch x 14-inch pillow form

Spring Lapghan & Pillow

Designs by *Diane Simpson*

Finished Size
Lapghan: 32 inches x 38 inches
Pillow: 17 inches x 18 inches

Materials
Lapghan
• Bernat Super Value medium (worsted) weight yarn (5 oz/275 yds/142g per skein):
  3 skeins color of choice
• Size K/10½/6.5mm crochet hook
• Size P/16/11.5mm afghan hook or size needed to obtain gauge
• Tapestry needle
Pillow
• Bernat Super Value medium (worsted) weight yarn (5 oz/275 yds/142g per skein):
  3 skeins color of choice
• Sizes H/8/5mm and I/9/5.5mm crochet hooks
• Size J/10/6mm afghan hook or size needed to obtain gauge
• Tapestry needle
• 14-inch x 18-inch pillow form

Lapghan

Gauge
Size P hook: 10 sts = 4 inches

Pattern Note
Weave in ends as work progresses.

Special Stitch
Tunisian knit stitch (tks): With yarn in back of work, insert hook to right of next vertical bar to back of work (*see Fig. 1*), yo, draw lp through.

Fig. 1
Tunisian Knit Stitch

Lapghan
Row 1 (RS): With size K hook, ch 80, change to size P hook, insert hook in 2nd ch from hook, yo, draw lp through, *insert hook in next ch, yo, draw lp through, rep from * across (*80 lps on hook*), to work lps off, yo, draw through 1 lp on hook, **yo, draw through 2 lps on hook, rep from ** until 1 lp rem on hook.

Row 2: Ch 1, sk first vertical bar, *tks (*see Special Stitch*), rep from * across to last vertical bar, insert hook so left vertical bar and back vertical bar are on left side of hook making straight edge, yo, draw lp through, to work lps off, yo, draw through 1 lp on hook, *yo, draw through 2 lps on hook, rep from * until 1 lp rem on hook.

Rows 3–80: Rep row 2. At end of last row, do not fasten off.

Edging

With size K hook, sl st in top lp of each horizontal bar across, ch 1, *working in ends of rows, *fpsl st *(see Stitch Guide)* around next horizontal bar, yo, draw through lp on hook, rep from * across to next corner, working in unworked lps on opposite side of starting ch, sl st in each ch across, ch 1, **fpsl st around next horizontal bar, yo, draw through lp on hook, rep from ** across to beg sl st, join with a sl st in beg sl st. Fasten off.

Pillow

Gauge

Size J hook: 14 sts = 4 inches

Pattern Notes

Weave in ends as work progresses.

Join with slip stitch as indicated unless otherwise stated.

Special Stitch

Tunisian knit stitch (tks): With yarn in back of work, insert hook to right of next vertical bar to back of work *(see Fig. 1, page 168)*, yo, draw lp through.

Pillow

Row 1 (WS): With size H hook, ch 134, sc in 2nd ch from hook, sc in each rem ch across, turn. *(133 sc)*

Row 2 (RS): With size J hook, insert hook in 2nd ch from hook, yo, draw lp through, *insert hook in next ch, yo, draw lp through, rep from * across *(133 lps on hook)*, to work lps off, yo, draw through 1 lp on hook, **yo, draw through 2 lps on hook, rep from ** until 1 lp rem on hook.

Row 3: Ch 1, sk first vertical bar, *****tks** (*see Special Stitch*), rep from * across to last vertical bar, insert hook so left vertical bar and back vertical bar are on left side of hook making straight edge, yo, draw lp through, to work lps off, yo, draw through 1 lp on hook, *yo, draw through 2 lps on hook, rep from * until 1 lp rem on hook.

Rows 4–41: Rep row 3.

Row 42: Change to size H hook, ch 1, sc in each horizontal bar across. Fasten off.

Edging

With size H hook, **join** (*see Pattern Notes*) yarn from front to back around **post** (*see Stitch Guide*) of first sc on row 42, **fpsl st** (*see Stitch Guide*) around post of each rem sc across. Fasten off.

Holding piece with starting ch at top, with size H hook, join yarn around first sc on row 1, fpsl st around post of each rem sc across. Fasten off.

Assembly

For back seam, sew ends of rows together through horizontal bars of each row.

Place piece on pillow.

Top Edging

Rnd 1 (RS): Holding piece with last row at top and back seam centered on 1 side of pillow form, flatten piece at corner, working through both thicknesses at same time in same sps as sl sts of Edging, and with size H hook, join yarn in same sp as first sl st of Edging, sl st in each sp across side, working around back between sts of first half of rnd, sl st in each horizontal bar across to joining sl st. Fasten off.

Rnd 2: With size I hook and working in sc of row 42, join yarn in first sc, ch 4, 3 tr in same sc, 3 tr in each rem sc around, sk beg ch-4, join in first tr. Fasten off.

Rnd 3: With size I hook and working in sl sts of rnd 1, join yarn with sc in first sl st at back seam, ch 3, sk next sl st, *sc in next sl st, ch 3, sk next sl st, rep from * around, join in first sc. Fasten off.

Lower Edging

Rnd 1 (RS): Holding piece with first row at top, flatten piece at corner, working through both thicknesses at same time and with size H hook, join yarn in same sp as sl st of Edging worked in, working in same sps as rem sl sts of Edging worked, sl st in each sp across side, working around back between sts of first half of rnd in sts of Edging, sl st in each horizontal bar across to joining sl st. Fasten off.

Rnd 2: With size I hook and working in sc of row 1, join yarn in first sc, ch 4, 3 tr in same sc, 3 tr in each rem sc around, sk beg ch-4, join in first tr. Fasten off.

Rnd 3: With size I hook and working in sl sts of rnd 1, join yarn with sc in first sl st at back seam, ch 3, sk next sl st, *sc in next sl st, ch 3, sk next sl st, rep from * around, join in first sc. Fasten off. ●

Mum Lapghan & Pillow
Continued from page 155

Hold joined Panels and Panel C with WS tog, top row of joined Panels corresponding to row 1 of Panel C, and joined Panels facing, working through both thicknesses at same time and with size J hook, join claret in sp between first 2 sts at left-hand edge, ch 2, work reverse sc in same sp, working from left to right in sp between sts and sk joining sts of Panels A and B, *ch 1, sk next sp, reverse sc in next sp, rep from * across, sl st in same sp as last reverse sc. Fasten off.

Referring to photo for placement and with matching yarn, sew flowers to Front.

Edging
Hold Front and Back with WS tog, Front facing and last row at top, working through both thicknesses at same time and with size J hook, join claret in sp between last 2 dc of last row at left-hand corner, ch 2, working left to right, work (reverse sc, ch 1) twice in same sp, working in sps between dc, *sk next sp, reverse sc in next sp, ch 1, rep from * across to last sp, (reverse sc, ch 1) twice in last sp, working across next side in ends of rows, **reverse sc in next row, ch 1, rep from ** across to next corner, working across next side in sps between sts, (reverse sc, ch 1) twice in first sp, ***sk next sp, reverse sc in next sp, ch 1, rep from *** across to last sp, (reverse sc, ch 1) twice in last sp, working across next side in ends of rows, ****reverse sc in next row, ch 1, rep from **** across to beg reverse sc, join in beg reverse sc. Fasten off. ●

Roaming Cables Lapghan & Pillow
Continued from page 159

Rnd 4: Ch 1, (pc, sc) in first st *(beg corner)*, sc in each of next 2 dc, [pc in next dc, sc in each of next 3 dc] 26 times, (sc, pc, sc) in next dc *(corner)*, sc in each of next 2 dc, [pc in next dc, sc in each of next 3 dc] 35 times, pc in next dc, sc in each of next 2 sc, (sc, pc, sc) in next dc *(corner)*, sc in each of next 2 dc, [pc in next dc, sc in each of next 3 dc] 26 times, (sc, pc, sc) in next dc *(corner)*, sc in each of next 2 dc, [pc in next dc, sc in each of next 3 dc] 35 times, pc in next sc, sc in each of next 2 sc, sc in same sc as beg pc, join in beg pc, turn. *(128 pc, 386 sc)*

Rnd 5: Ch 3, 2 dc in first st *(beg corner)*, *dc in each st across to pc in next corner, 3 dc in pc *(corner)*, rep from * twice, dc in each st across to beg ch-3, join in 3rd ch of beg ch-3. Fasten off.

Pillow
Gauge
Size L hook: 8 sts = 4 inches

Pattern Notes
Weave in ends as work progresses.

Chain-2 at beginning of rows counts as first half double crochet unless otherwise stated.

Chain-3 at beginning of rows counts as first double crochet unless otherwise stated.

Special Stitch
Popcorn (pc): 4 sc in indicated st, remove hook, insert hook from back to front through first and 4th sc, yo, draw lp through sc.

Pillow
Front/Back
Make 2.
Center Panel
Row 1 (RS): With size L hook, ch 25, working in back bumps of chs, hdc in 3rd ch from hook *(beg 2 sk chs count as a hdc)*, hdc in each rem ch across, turn. *(24 hdc)*

Row 2: Ch 2 *(see Pattern Notes)*, hdc in each hdc across, hdc in 2nd ch of beg 2 sk chs, turn.

Row 3: Ch 2, hdc in next hdc, *sk next 2 hdc on 2nd row below, **fpdc** *(see Stitch Guide)* around each of next 2 hdc on 2nd row below, working in front of fpdc just made, fpdc around each sk hdc on 2nd row **, on working row, sk hdc behind fpdc, hdc in each of next 4 hdc, rep from * twice, ending last rep at **, hdc in last hdc, hdc in 2nd ch of beg ch-2, turn.

Row 4: Ch 2, hdc in each hdc across, hdc in 2nd ch of beg ch-2, turn.

Note: On following rows, always sk sts on working row behind fpdc.

Row 5: Ch 2, hdc in next hdc, *sk next 2 fpdc, fpdc around each of next 2 fpdc, working in front of fpdc just made, fpdc around each sk fpdc **, hdc in each of next 4 hdc, rep from * twice, ending last rep at **, hdc in last hdc, hdc in 2nd ch of beg ch-2, turn.

Row 6: Rep row 4.

Row 7: Ch 2, *fpdc around each of next 2 fpdc, hdc in each of next 2 hdc, fpdc around each of next 2 fpdc**, rep from * twice, ending last rep at **, hdc in 2nd ch of beg ch-2, turn.

Row 8: Rep row 4.

Row 9: Ch 2, *fpdc around each of next 2 fpdc, hdc in each of next 2 hdc, fpdc around each of next 2 fpdc **, rep from * twice, ending last rep at **, hdc in 2nd ch of beg ch-2, turn.

Row 10: Rep row 4.

Row 11: Ch 2, hdc in next hdc, *fpdc around each of next 4 fpdc, hdc in each of next 4 hdc, rep from * once, fpdc around each of next 4 fpdc, hdc in last hdc, hdc in 2nd ch of beg ch-2, turn.

Row 12: Rep row 4.

Row 13: Ch 2, hdc in next hdc, *sk next 2 fpdc, fpdc around each of next 2 fpdc, working in front of 2 fpdc just made, fpdc around each sk fpdc **, hdc in each of next 4 hdc, rep from * twice, ending last rep at **, hdc in last hdc, hdc in 2nd ch of beg ch-2, turn.

Row 14: Rep row 4.

Row 15: Ch 2, hdc in next hdc, *sk next 2 fpdc, fpdc around each of next 2 fpdc, working in front of 2 fpdc just made, fpdc around each sk fpdc **, hdc in each of next 4 hdc, rep from * twice, ending last rep at **, hdc in last hdc, hdc in 2nd ch of beg ch-2, turn.

Rows 16–39: [Rep rows 8–15 consecutively] 3 times. At end of last row, fasten off.

Right Side Panel

Row 1 (RS): Hold piece with RS facing and starting ch to right, with size K hook, join yarn with sc in end of row 1, working in

ends of rows, work 43 sc evenly sp across, turn. *(44 sc)*

Row 2: Ch 1, **fpsc** *(see Stitch Guide)* around each sc across, turn.

Row 3: Ch 3 *(see Pattern Notes)*, dc in each sc across, turn.

Row 4: Ch 1, sc in each of first 2 dc, ***pc** *(see Special Stitches)* in next dc, sc in each of next 3 dc, rep from * 9 times, sc in next dc, sc in 3rd ch of beg ch-3, turn. *(11 pc, 24 sc)*

Row 5: Ch 3, dc in each st across. Fasten off.

Left Side Panel

Row 1 (RS): Hold piece with RS facing and row 39 to right, with size K hook, join yarn with sc in end of row 39, working in ends of rows, work 43 sc evenly spaced across, turn. *(44 sc)*

Row 2: Ch 1, fpsc around each sc across, turn.

Row 3: Ch 3, dc in each sc across, turn.

Row 4: Ch 1, sc in first dc, *pc in next dc, sc in each of next 2 dc, rep from * 9 times, pc in next dc, sc in next dc, sc in 3rd ch of beg ch-3, turn. *(11 pc, 24 sc)*

Row 5: Ch 3, dc in each st across. Fasten off.

Assembly

Hold Front and Back with WS facing, with tapestry needle and working in **back lps** *(see Stitch Guide)*, sew 3 sides tog. Insert pillow form. Sew rem side closed. ●

Rainbow Lapghan & Pillow
Continued from page 167

Assembly

For large front and back squares, 4 Motifs are joined tog in 2 rows of 2 Motifs for each large square. To join Motifs, hold 2 Motifs with RS tog, join soft white in ch-2 sp of right-hand corner, ch 1, sc in same sp, working in **back lps** *(see Stitch Guide)*, sc in each dc across to next corner ch-2 sp, sc in corner ch-2 sp. Fasten off. Join 2 additional Motifs in same manner. Join rem 4 Motifs in same manner.

Border

Rnd 1: Hold 1 large square with RS facing, join soft white in upper right-hand corner ch-2 sp, ch 3, (dc, ch 2, 2 dc) in same sp *(beg corner)*, *dc in each dc and each ch sp on each side of each joining seam across to next outer corner ch-2 sp **, (2 dc, ch 2, 2 dc) in corner ch-2 sp *(corner)*, rep from * 3 times, ending last rep at **, join in 3rd ch of beg ch-3.

Rnd 2: Ch 1, sc in same ch as joining, sc in each dc around, working 3 sc in each corner ch-2 sp, join in beg sc.

Work Border in same manner on 2nd large square.

Edging

Rnd 1: Hold large squares with WS tog, working through both thicknesses at same

time, join soft white in 2nd sc in upper right-hand corner, ch 1, sc in same sc as joining, working around 3 sides, sc in each sc, on 4th side, working in sc on front square only, sc in each rem sc to beg sc, join in beg sc. Fasten off.

Rnd 2: Join Eden green in beg sc, ch 3, 2 dc in same sc, 3 dc in each rem sc around, join in 3rd ch of beg ch-3.

Rnd 3: Ch 3, dc in each dc around, join in 3rd ch of beg ch-3. Fasten off.

Finishing

Insert pillow form. With tapestry needle and soft white, sew opening closed. ●

Stitch Guide

Abbreviations

beg	begin/beginning
bpdc	back post double crochet
bpsc	back post single crochet
bptr	back post treble crochet
CC	contrasting color
ch	chain stitch
ch-	refers to chain or space previously made (i.e., ch-1 space)
ch sp	chain space
cl	cluster
cm	centimeter(s)
dc	double crochet
dec	decrease/decreases/decreasing
dtr	double treble crochet
fpdc	front post double crochet
fpsc	front post single crochet
fptr	front post treble crochet
g	gram(s)
hdc	half double crochet
inc	increase/increases/increasing
lp(s)	loop(s)
MC	main color
mm	millimeter(s)
oz	ounce(s)
pc	popcorn
rem	remain/remaining
rep	repeat(s)
rnd(s)	round(s)
RS	right side
sc	single crochet
sk	skip(ped)
sl st	slip stitch
sp(s)	space(s)
st(s)	stitch(es)
tog	together
tr	treble crochet
trtr	triple treble crochet
WS	wrong side
yd(s)	yard(s)
yo	yarn over

Chain—ch: Yo, pull through lp on hook.

Slip stitch—sl st: Insert hook in st, pull through both lps on hook.

Single crochet—sc: Insert hook in st, yo, pull through st, yo, pull through both lps on hook.

Front post stitch—fp: Back post stitch—bp: When working post st, insert hook from right to left around post st on previous row.

Back   Front

Post of Stitch

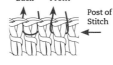

Front loop—front lp Back loop— back lp

Front Loop   Back Loop

Half double crochet—hdc: Yo, insert hook in st, yo, pull through st, yo, pull through all 3 lps on hook.

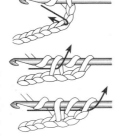

Double crochet—dc: Yo, insert hook in st, yo, pull through st, [yo, pull through 2 lps] twice.

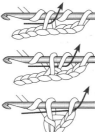

Example of 2-tr dec

Change colors: Drop first color; with 2nd color, pull through last 2 lps of st.

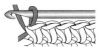

Treble crochet—tr: Yo twice, insert hook in st, yo, pull through st, [yo, pull through 2 lps] 3 times.

Double treble crochet—dtr: Yo 3 times, insert hook in st, yo, pull through st, [yo, pull through 2 lps], 4 times.

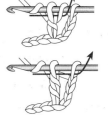

Single crochet decrease (sc dec): (Insert hook, yo, draw lp through) in each of the sts indicated, yo, draw through all lps on hook.

Half double crochet decrease (hdc dec): (Yo, insert hook, yo, draw lp through) in each of the sts indicated, yo, draw through all lps on hook.

Double crochet decrease (dc dec): (Yo, insert hook, yo, draw loop through, draw through 2 lps on hook) in each of the sts indicated, yo, draw through all lps on hook.

Treble crochet decrease (tr dec): Holding back last lp of each st, tr in each of the sts indicated, yo, pull through all lps on hook.

US		UK
sl st (slip stitch)	=	sc (single crochet)
sc (single crochet)	=	dc (double crochet)
hdc (half double crochet)	=	htr (half treble crochet)
dc (double crochet)	=	tr (treble crochet)
tr (treble crochet)	=	dtr (double treble crochet)
dtr (double treble crochet)	=	ttr (triple treble crochet)
skip	=	miss

Special Thanks

....

Cynthia Adams
Manly Afghan 14

Elaine Bartlett
Travel Pillows 18

Pam Bruce
Pineapple
Bathroom Set 128

Donna Childs
Colorful Dolls 122
Hearts Delight 90
Pop Top Mittens 10

Rhonda Dodds
Checkers Game 119

Katherine Eng
Tweed Granny Rug 136

Nazanin Fard
Felted Necklace 46
Man's Lapghan 24

Lisa Gentry
Man's Hat & Scarf 12

Lillian Gimmelli
Delicate Lace
Table Runner 132

Christine Grazioso-Moody
Sunshine Afghan 84

Kyleigh Hawke
Peachy Clean 140

Lucille LaFlamme
Sunday Pink 80

Jewdy Lambert
Angora Scarf
& Gloves 55
Baby Boy Sheriff 78
Camo Socks 20
Flower & Ruffle Trim
Hat & Scarf 60
Man's Slippers 8
Updated Ruffled Scarf 50

Sheila Leslie
Blue/White Hat
& Scarf 22
Lemon Drops 86

Susan Lowman
Basketweave
Eyeglass Case 44

Lisa Marchand Harris
Apple Tea Cozy
& Coaster 142

Pamela Noel
Dust Mitt 134

Shirley Patterson
Boy Blue Sunday Suit 74
Dainty Slippers 48
Serenity Blue Dress 70

Diane Simpson
Man's Black Hat 28
Spring Lapghan
& Pillow 168

Darla Sims
Bath Mitts 114
Funky Hat 112
Roaming Cables
Lapghan & Pillow 156
Santa Toilet Seat Cover 116
Quick as a Wink Jacket 39

Rena V. Stevens
Mum Lapghan & Pillow 152
Man' s Diamond
Lapghan & Pillow 160

Brenda Stratton
Jewelry Roll 58

Erica Taylor
Rasta Hat 26

Emma Willey
Scrub a Dub 138

Glenda Winkleman
Hoodie Scarf 52
Rainbow Lapghan
& Pillow 164
Man's Camo Hat & Scarf 16

Lori Zeller
Felted Purse 40